THE SON OF GOD

JESUS
THE MIRACLES OF JESUS
THE PARABLES OF JESUS
THE TWELVE DISCIPLES

BARBOUR
PUBLISHING, INC.
Uhrichsville, Ohio

© 2001 by Barbour Publishing, Inc.

ISBN 1-58660-133-4

Jesus by Dan Larsen. © 1989 by Barbour Publishing, Inc.
The Miracles of Jesus by Ellyn Sanna. © 2000 by Barbour Publishing, Inc.
The Parables of Jesus by Ellyn Sanna. © 2000 by Barbour Publishing, Inc..
The Twelve Disciples by Ellyn Sanna. © 2001 by Barbour Publishing, Inc.

Published by Barbour Publishing, Inc., P.O. Box 719, Uhrichsville, Ohio 44683
http://www.barbourbooks.com

Member of the
Evangelical Christian
Publishers Association

Printed in the United States of America.

CONTENTS

CONTENTS

JESUS

THE SON OF GOD

by Dan Larsen

CHAPTER 1

We had been fishing all morning, my brother Andrew and I, on Lake Galilee. Though our nets had been in the water for many hours, our catch was small. About midday we hauled in our nets and rowed to shore. There we sat in the boat, mending and washing our nets.

We had not been at this long when I heard someone call my name. "Simon." I looked up. On the shore stood a man I had never seen before. I started to ask how He knew me when He said, "Follow Me, Simon, and you, Andrew. From now on you will be fishers of men."

I never looked at Andrew. I did not know, or care, what he was thinking just then. I was looking at the man. He wore a robe that came to His ankles. By His powerful shoulders, I could see that He was a house builder. But His face! Such strength I have never seen in any man. Even more than this, there was such authority in His gaze and voice that as I stood in my boat looking at Him, I could say nothing. His eyes shone like all the stars in the heavens and seemed to stare right through my eyes into the depths of my soul.

I will never forget what happened next. I stood in my boat with my net, the only things I had ever owned. Fishing was my only past and my only future. I had no more desire to leave that life behind than I did to die. But when the man on the shore said, "Follow Me," I clambered out of my boat and splashed to shore. My heart was pounding; my knees trembling. The man turned and walked down the shore. I followed Him, like a child, not once looking back at my boat.

It was only then that I realized my brother Andrew was with me. He, too, had felt the call, felt it deep in his heart, and he had obeyed, too.

The man walked along the shore, Andrew and I at His heels, until He came to two other brothers in their boat. "James and John," the man called, "come with Me." At once, the men dropped their nets, climbed out of the boat, and came to us.

We followed this man throughout Galilee. Here and there, He called more men to Him. Before long there were twelve of us. Over the next three years, we would follow this man all over Judea. We would see and hear things such as we had never seen or heard before. We would see the sick made well, the lame walk, the deaf speak, the blind see, and the dead raised to life. We would see the very kingdom of heaven come down to earth! The whole world, all that is in it and all that will ever be, would be changed forever by the life of this one man.

I saw and heard these things, I and the other eleven men with me those three years. Not only we twelve, but many, many people all through the land of Judea saw and heard.

The stories that are told of this man are true. They are not tales of imagination. They are the accounts of those who were there, who saw, who heard, who knew. I was with Him wherever He went for those three years. I came to understand Who He was. I grew to love Him with all my heart and soul and strength. And He gave me a new name. "You are Peter, the rock," He said. "And on this Rock I will build My church."

He called us disciples. When He left us He said, "Go into all the world and make everyone My disciples."

I have not written of these things before. Now I write because I must tell this story, first what I heard from many people who knew Him before I, then what I saw and heard for myself when I was with Him. This is the story of Jesus Christ, the Son of God, the Savior of the world.

CHAPTER 2

It began in the city of Nazareth when Herod was king of Judea. In Nazareth lived a young woman named Mary. She was not yet married but was engaged to a man named Joseph.

One night she was startled awake. There in her room stood an angel. "My name is Gabriel," he said. "Peace be with you. The Lord is with you and has richly blessed you." Mary was trembling.

"Do not fear," the angel said. "You will become pregnant and give birth to a son, and you will name Him Jesus. He will be called the Son of God. And there will be no end to His kingdom."

"How can this be?" said Mary. "I am not married. I am a virgin."

God's power will come upon you," the angel said. "There is nothing that God cannot do."

"I am the Lord's servant," Mary said. "Let it be done to me as you have said."

It was many months before Joseph and Mary were to be married. Before that time, Joseph learned that Mary was pregnant. He decided to tell her privately that he would not marry her, since he did not wish her shame to be known to everyone.

But one night in a dream an angel came to him and said, "Joseph, do not be afraid to take Mary as your wife. She has not shamed you. It is by the power of God that she is pregnant. She will have a son, Whom you are to name Jesus, and He will save people from their sins. This is the child spoken of by the prophet who said, 'Behold, the virgin shall bear a son, Who will be called Immanuel, or God With Us.' "

So Mary and Joseph were married. Soon after, Emperor Augustus of Rome ordered a census, a count of the people living in the huge Roman Empire. All the people had to return to the place of their birth to be registered for the census. Joseph and Mary had to go to the town of Bethlehem, where their families came from.

They came to Bethlehem late one night. The inns were all full. It was cold, and Mary was about to give birth. They found a small stable where some animals were kept, and there Mary gave birth to Jesus. She wrapped Him in cloths and laid Him in a manger.

In a pasture near Bethlehem, some shepherds were spending the night with their flocks. Just after Jesus was born, an angel came to the shepherds and said, "I bring good news, which will bring great joy to all people. This very day in the city of David your Savior was born, Christ the Lord. You will find a baby wrapped in cloths and lying in a manger."

And suddenly it became bright as day. Great armies of angels joined the first angel. They all sang, "Glory to God in the highest heaven, and peace on earth to those with whom He is pleased."

The shepherds hurried into Bethlehem, where they found the baby. They told Mary and Joseph what the angel said, then they returned to their flocks, singing and praising God.

After about two years, Mary and Joseph returned to Nazareth. There the child, Jesus, grew to manhood. He helped his father, who was a house builder. Jesus grew strong in body and in wisdom.

When Jesus was about thirty years old, a man named John came out of the wilderness near Jerusalem. "Repent of your sins and be baptized!" he cried to the people. He went to the Jordan River, south of Lake Galilee, where he baptized people in the water. Many people came to him. "He is the Lord's holy prophet!" they said.

We fishermen of Lake Galilee began hearing of John— John the Baptist, as he was called. "Could he be the Messiah?" people asked. When John heard this, he answered, "I am not the One you are looking for. I baptize you in water for repentance. There is One coming after me Who is much mightier than I am. I am not worthy to tie His sandals. He will baptize you in the Holy Spirit and in fire. I am only the one the prophet Isaiah spoke of when he said, 'Someone is shouting in the desert. Prepare a road for the Lord! Make a straight path for Him to travel!' The One coming after me will gather His wheat into His barn, but He will burn the chaff in a fire that never goes out."

Jesus came to the Jordan. When John saw Him he said, "I should be baptized by You. Yet You have come to me!"

"Let it be so," said Jesus. "We must do all that God requires."

So John baptized Him. Just as Jesus came out of the water He saw heaven open, and God's Spirit came down to Him in the form of a dove that rested on Him. Then a voice said, "You are My own dear Son, in Whom I have delighted."

Now the Spirit of God led Jesus into the desert. There He stayed, praying day and night. He ate no food all this time. After forty days, Satan came to Him and said, "If you are the Son of God, command these stones to turn into bread."

Jesus said, "It is written, 'Man cannot live on bread alone, but needs every word that God speaks.' "

Then Satan said, "Come with me." He led Jesus to Jerusalem, where he climbed to the top of the temple. There Satan said, "If You are the Son of God, jump off from here. For it is written, 'God will command His angels to guard You. They will hold You up so that not even Your feet will be hurt on the stones.' "

Jesus replied, "It is also written, 'Do not put the Lord your God to the test.' "

Then Satan took Jesus to the top of a tall mountain. There he said, "Do You see all those kingdoms below? I will give You all those if You kneel down and worship me."

Jesus said, "Get away from Me, Satan! It is written, 'Worship the Lord your God and serve only Him.' "

Hearing this, Satan fled over the desert. Jesus was very weak from having gone so long without food, but angels came to Him and helped Him down the mountain.

He went to live in a city called Capernaum, near Lake Galilee. Now filled with the Spirit and power of God, He began to preach to people in the synagogues. "Turn away from your sins," He said. "The kingdom of heaven is near."

CHAPTER 4

It was then that He came to us on Lake Galilee. We followed Him into the synagogues, where He spoke of a coming kingdom. We did not understand everything, but we were drawn to Him. There was power in every word He spoke. People listened to Him in amazement. "He speaks with such authority!" we heard people say. "We have never heard anything like this!"

Three days after Jesus had come to us at Lake Galilee, we went to the city of Cana, where we had been invited to a wedding. The house was full of people, and Jesus' mother was there. Before long, she came to Jesus. "They have no more wine," she said.

"Why have you told Me this?" He asked quietly. "My time has not yet come."

Andrew and I looked at each other. What did this mean?

Then Jesus' mother turned away and said to the servants of the house, "Do whatever He tells you." The servants came to Jesus, waiting for Him to speak.

Finally He pointed to six stone water jars, each able to hold about thirty gallons. "Fill those with water," He said. "Then draw some out and take it to the man in charge of the feast."

We watched as a servant dipped some water out and

went to the man. The servant said something to the man, then handed the dipper to him. As the man took a sip, his eyes went wide. He stared at the servant, then at the dipper, then at the stone jars. Then he beamed and clapped the servant on the back. Now the man walked over to the bridegroom, who was standing near us. "Sir," the man said, "everyone else serves the best wine first and the cheapest after everyone has drunk freely. But you have saved the best wine until now!"

No one except the servants and us disciples knew where this wine had come from. We were so astounded we could hardly speak. "Who is this man?" we said to one another. "He must be sent from God! No man could have this power, if it were not given him by God Himself."

After this wedding, we went with Jesus and His mother and brothers to Capernaum and stayed there for a few days. The days of the Passover festival were drawing near, and we were going to travel to Jerusalem to celebrate this festival.

In Jerusalem, the first thing Jesus did was go to the temple, the holy place of Jerusalem, the place of worship. But we were not prepared for what we saw inside!

There were cattle and sheep and cages filled with pigeons, and tables filled with coins throughout the temple. People were everywhere. Men were crying out, "Buy here! Buy here!" The din of bickering and squabbling echoed off the tall stone pillars and walls, as in a hollow cavern.

Jesus stopped short on seeing this. His eyes glinted like

steel as He looked around, His fists clenched. Then He moved. He wrenched a cord of rope from a heavy curtain. Using this as a whip, He drove the cattle and sheep across the floor and out of the temple. Bawling and bleating, the animals stampeded toward the doors. Men screamed and ran for safety.

Then Jesus grabbed the massive wooden tables and flung them to the floor with a fury that seemed to crack the very stones under our feet. Silver and gold coins rang across the floor.

No one tried to stop Him. All stood wide-eyed and open-mouthed as this powerful figure cleared the temple. Soon it was still.

Jesus pointed at the sellers. His voice boomed in the now-silent temple. "This is My Father's house," He said. "But you have made it a hideout for thieves!"

The priests and the teachers of the Law were in the temple. They were furious with Jesus. But now a crowd was gathering. People poured in through the doors. They had seen the stampeding animals and were curious. A murmur rose up among the people, then grew to a roar. "Praise the God of the heavens!" they shouted. "This man comes in the name of God!"

The priests stayed in the shadows of the temple, afraid of Jesus and the excitement He stirred up among the people. They did not dare say a word.

During the days of the Passover festival, Jesus taught in the temple, and many came to Him to be healed. With a word, He healed all their diseases. More and more people came into the temple, many of them saying that Jesus was the Messiah, the Promised One. But fear and hatred grew in the priests and the teachers.

One teacher, though, must have heard something in the words of Jesus that made Him hunger to know more. He came to the house where we stayed one night. "I am Nicodemus," he said to Jesus. "I am a leader of the Pharisees. We know that You are a teacher Who has come from God, for no one could do the miracles You have done unless he had the power of God."

"I tell you the truth," Jesus said, "unless a man be born again, he cannot see the kingdom of God."

Nicodemus frowned. "How can a man be born again?" he asked.

"You must be born of water and the Spirit," Jesus said. "You are born physically from human parents, but you must be born spiritually by the Spirit. The wind blows wherever it wishes, and you listen to its sound, but you know not where it comes from or where it is going. It is like that with everyone who is born of the Spirit."

"How can this be?" asked Nicodemus.

"You are a teacher of Israel," Jesus said, "and you do not know this? You teachers do not believe Me when I tell you about the things of this world. How will you ever believe Me when I tell you about the things of heaven?

"As Moses lifted up the bronze snake in the desert, so must the Son of Man be lifted up, so that everyone who believes in Him may have life eternal. For God loved the world so much that He gave His only Son, so that whoever believes in Him should not die, but have life eternal."

Nicodemus went away into the night, puzzled over what Jesus had said.

When the Passover festival was over, we left Jerusalem and went into the countryside, where Jesus' disciples baptized many people in the Jordan. After two days, we went to Cana in Galilee, where Jesus had turned the water into wine. Here the people recognized Jesus, for many of them had been to the festival in Jerusalem. Word of Jesus' teaching and His miracles had spread quickly. Crowds gathered around us as we walked through the dusty streets.

We had been here a few days when a court officer from Capernaum came to see Jesus at the hour of seven one evening. The man was wringing his hands. "Sir," he said, "my son is dying. Please come with me before it is too late."

"Go," Jesus said. "Your son lives!"

A look of wonder came over the man's face. Straightening his shoulders, he said, "I believe! I will go, as You say."

We later learned that the boy became well at that very hour. The man and all his family believed in Jesus.

We traveled to Capernaum, where Jesus went into the synagogue on the Sabbath to teach. One of these days as Jesus was teaching the crowd, a man came forward. We all drew back in terror at the sight of him. His eyes were blazing with a strange fire. His lips were twisted in a bestial grin. Suddenly he screamed, "What do you want with us, Jesus of Nazareth? Have you come to destroy us? I know Who You are. You are the Holy One of God!"

The crowd was hushed. Everyone stared in horror at this raging man. Jesus stood in front of him. The man was shaking and foaming at the mouth. His hands clutched like talons at the empty air. He seemed ready to erupt, like a volcano. We gasped. What would he do? Attack Jesus?

But Jesus pointed straight at the man. The man threw his head back as if to let out another shriek. "Be still!" came Jesus' voice. There was danger in those words, as sharp as a sword. The man suddenly stood as if he were locked in a vise. Then Jesus said, "Come out of him!"

Suddenly the man fell to the floor, as if thrown by invisible hands. Jesus helped him up. Now the man sobbed and praised God. The evil look in his eyes was gone.

Shouts of praise went up from the crowd, and many

people stared in wonder at Jesus. "What authority and power are in His words!" we heard some say. "He commands, and even evil spirits tremble before Him and obey! Praise the name of God!"

People went everywhere telling of Jesus. His fame spread like fire through the whole region. We went all through Galilee, where Jesus taught in the synagogues. Many people came to believe in Him. He healed the sick, made the blind see, the lame walk, and cast out evil spirits. In every city we entered, the people thronged around us to see Jesus and hear Him speak.

We began to stay out in the wilderness so we could have some peace from the crowds. But even in the wilderness, the people found and followed us. They came from Galilee and the Decapolis, from Jerusalem and all of Judea, even from Syria.

One day Jesus went up a mountain alone. He stayed there all night, praying. Very early the next morning, He woke us. Of the men following Him, He appointed twelve to be his apostles, or disciples. He appointed me—Simon— my brother Andrew, the brothers James and John, who were sons of Zebedee, Philip, Bartholomew (also called Nathanael), Thomas, Matthew, James the son of Alphaeus, Judas Thaddaeus, Simon of Cana, and Judas Iscariot.

Then He took the twelve of us to the top of the mountain, told us to sit down, and began to teach us.

"Happy are you who are poor, for the kingdom of God is yours," He said.

"Happy are you who mourn, for God will comfort you.

"Happy are you who are humble, for you will receive what God has promised.

"Happy are you who show mercy, for God will show mercy to you.

"Happy are you who are pure in heart, for you will see God.

"Happy are you who work for peace, for God will call you His children.

"Happy are you who are persecuted for doing what God requires, for the kingdom of heaven belongs to you.

"Happy are you when people insult you and tell lies about you because you are My followers. Be happy and glad, for a great reward is kept for you in heaven. This is how the prophets who lived before you were persecuted."

The morning passed, the afternoon came, and still we sat with Jesus. His face shone as He spoke to us.

"You are like light for the world," He said. "And no one lights a lamp and puts it under a bowl. Instead, he puts it on a lampstand, where it gives light for everyone in the house. In the same way, your light must shine before people, so they will see the good things you do and praise your Father in heaven.

"Do not think that I have come to do away with the Law

of Moses and the teachings of the prophets. I have come to make their teachings come true. Remember that as long as heaven and earth last, not the smallest detail of the Law will be done away with—not until the end of all things. You will be able to enter the kingdom of heaven only if you are more faithful than the teachers of the Law and the Pharisees in doing what God requires.

"You have been told that anyone who commits murder will be brought to trial. But now I tell you that whoever is angry with his brothers will be brought to trial; whoever says to his brother, 'You good-for-nothing!' will be brought before the council; and whoever says to his brother, 'You worthless fool!' will be in danger of going to hell. So if you are about to offer a gift to God at the altar and you remember that your brother has something against you, go at once and make peace with your brother, and then come back and offer your gift to God.

"You have been told not to commit adultery. But now I tell you that anyone who lusts for a woman is guilty of committing adultery with her in his heart.

"You have heard it said, 'An eye for an eye, and a tooth for a tooth,' But now I tell you, do not take revenge on someone who wrongs you. If someone slaps you on the right cheek, let him slap you on the left cheek also. And if someone sues you for your shirt, let him have your coat, as well.

"When you give something to a needy person, do not

make a show of it. Do it privately so that even your closest friend will not know. And your Father, Who sees what you do in private, will reward you. And when you pray, do not stand in the streets. Go to your room, close the door, and pray to your Father, Who is unseen. And do not use a lot of meaningless words. Your Father already knows what you need. This, then, is how you should pray. 'Our Father in heaven, may Your holy name be honored. May Your kingdom come. May Your will be done on earth as it is in heaven. Give us today the food we need. Forgive us the wrongs we have done, as we forgive the wrongs that others do to us. Keep us from temptation, and keep us safe from the Evil One."

Every word Jesus spoke became etched in my heart forever.

CHAPTER 6

When we came down from the mountain, we were met by great crowds of people who followed us into Capernaum, where we stayed that night. The next morning we set out for the city of Nain. We left Capernaum very early and walked all day. Toward evening we came to the city gates of Nain.

As we were about to enter, a large crowd of people came out from the city. Many of them wept. On the men's shoulders was a young boy stretched out on a bier, his face as pale as death. A woman walked beside the bier, wailing aloud.

We asked one of the men what had happened. "This woman's only child has died," he said sadly. "She is a widow and has no one left."

When Jesus heard this, a tender look came over His face. He looked at the woman as if He would weep, too. He walked toward the bier. "Do not weep," He said. Everyone stopped. They stared at Jesus as He came up to the dead boy. "Young man," Jesus said, "I tell you, get up!"

A gasp went up from the crowd. The boy was sitting up! "A great prophet has appeared!" came a shout. "God has come to save His people!" The woman held her son tightly as great sobs of joy shook her.

This story spread quickly throughout that region. We

went with Jesus to city after city. We were followed every-where. In the cities, we were so pressed by crowds that some-times we could not even sit down to eat. More and more, Jesus would go to Lake Galilee and sit in a boat just off-shore to speak to the crowds. He would speak in parables. Many people would only wonder what He meant, but oth-ers understood.

"Once there was a man who went out to sow grain," Jesus said. "As he scattered the seed, some of it fell along the path, where the birds ate it. Some fell on rocky ground. The seeds soon sprouted, but because the soil was shal-low, the plants did not grow deep roots and were burned by the sun. Some seed fell among thorn bushes, which grew up and choked the plants. But some seed fell in good soil and bore grain. Some had a hundred grains, others sixty, and others thirty. Listen, then, if you have ears."

When the crowds had left, we disciples asked Jesus why He spoke to the people only in parables. He answered, "Be-cause these people look, but do not see, and listen, but do not hear or understand. The prophet Isaiah spoke of these people when he said, 'They will listen, but not understand. They will look, but not see, because their minds are dull, and they have stopped up their ears and have closed their eyes. Otherwise, their eyes would see, their ears would hear, their minds would understand, and they would turn to Me, says God, and I would heal them.'

"As for you," Jesus said, "your eyes see and your ears hear. This is what the parable of the sower means. Those who hear My message but do not understand are like the seed that fell on the path. The Evil One comes and snatches away what was sown in them. The seeds that fell on rocky ground are those who receive the message gladly as soon as they hear it. But it does not sink deep into them, and they do not last long. When trouble comes, they give up at once. The seeds that fell among thorn bushes are those who hear the message but allow the worries of life and the love of riches to choke the message. And the seeds sown in good soil are those who hear and understand. They are the ones who bear fruit."

Jesus told many other parables. "The kingdom of heaven is like a mustard seed," He said. "It is the smallest of seeds, but it grows into the biggest of plants. It becomes a tree, so that birds make their nests in its branches.

"The kingdom of heaven is like this. A man is looking for fine pearls. When he finds one that is unusually fine, he goes and sells everything he has and buys that pearl.

"The kingdom of heaven is like this. Fishermen throw their net out and catch all kinds of fish. When the net is full, they pull it to shore and sit down to divide the fish. The good ones go into buckets, and the worthless ones are thrown away. It will be like this at the end of the age. The angels will go out and gather up the evil people from among the good and will throw them into the fire."

When it began to grow dark, we disciples sent the crowds home. Then we were alone with Jesus. We all got into the boat with Him to go to the other side of the lake. Jesus quickly fell asleep in the boat. About halfway across, the wind picked up, and the waves rose. Soon we were in a violent windstorm. The waves began washing over the sides of the boat. Frantically, we worked to keep the boat afloat, bailing out water and bracing ourselves against the smashing waves. All through this, Jesus slept.

Now we were sure we would be drowned. I shook Jesus. "Master!" I cried. "Do you not care that we are about to drown?"

Jesus awoke and frowned at me. "Why are you afraid?" He asked. "Where is your faith?" Then He stood up in the pitching boat. We all stared at Him in wonder. His voice came like thunder. "Be still!"

Immediately the wind stopped. A great calm settled over the water. Jesus calmly went back to sleep again.

"Who is this man?" we said. "Even the winds and waves obey His commands!" And I wondered if there was anything He couldn't do.

Chapter 7

Soon we went to Jerusalem to celebrate a feast of the Jews. In Jerusalem we came upon a man lying on a mat by the street. He seemed very ill. Jesus said, "You have been here long."

The man stared up at Jesus. "How did You know that?" he asked. "I have been sick for many years. I cannot walk very far. I am too weak."

Jesus' face shone with a soft light. "Get up!" He said to the man. "Pick up your mat and walk."

The man's eyes opened wide, but he took a deep breath and stood up. He stared at Jesus open mouthed, and tears came to his eyes. Slowly he picked up his mat and walked away, speechless.

People were staring. "We must go quickly," Jesus said. We got away before a crowd could gather.

About two days later, the priests from the temple came to us. Their faces were grave as they spoke to Jesus. "On the past Sabbath we saw a man carrying his sleeping mat," they said. "When we told him it is against our Law to carry his mat on a Sabbath, he said that a certain man told him to carry it."

One of the priests pointed at Jesus. The priest was

bristling. "That man was You!" he said. "You are a Jew. Have you no regard for our Law?"

Jesus said, "My Father is always working, and I, too, must work."

"Your Father!" said a priest through clenched teeth. "You are saying God is Your Father. For this You deserve death!"

The priests gathered in front of Jesus, their fists clenched, their faces flushed. But they cowered together in a knot, as a pack of hounds before a lion.

Though Jesus spoke calmly, His words seemed to fly through the air like arrows toward the group of priests. "I tell you the truth," Jesus said. "The Son does only what He sees His Father doing. For the Father loves the Son and shows Him even greater things to do than this. You will be amazed. Just as the Father raises the dead and gives them life, in the same way the Son gives life to those He wants to. Nor does the Father Himself judge anyone." Here Jesus looked sharply at the priest. "He has given His Son the full right to judge. And whoever does not honor the Son does not honor the Father who sent Him. I am telling you the truth. Whoever hears My words and believes in Him Who sent Me has eternal life. He will not be judged but has already passed from death to life. The Father Himself testifies on My behalf. You have never heard His voice or seen His face, and you do not keep His message in your hearts, for you do not believe in the One He sent. You study the

Scriptures, because you think that in them you will find eternal life. And these very Scriptures speak about Me! Yet you are not willing to come to Me in order to have life."

This made the priests all the more furious, but they said nothing.

Soon we left Jerusalem and went north to Nazareth. From there we went north again and sailed across Lake Galilee to a wilderness region outside the city of Bethsaida. Here Jesus hoped to rest for a little while.

But somehow people knew we had come. Even in the wilderness, they flocked to Jesus like lost sheep. They brought their sick and lame and blind. Jesus healed many, many people that day. Then He spoke to them about the kingdom of heaven.

The day passed and night came. Jesus drew us disciples aside. "Where can we get food for these people?" He asked. As I looked at Him, I wondered if He already knew the answer.

Philip said, "Master, there must be five thousand men here, not counting the women and children. All we have are two small fish and five loaves of bread!"

"Send the people home where they can eat," I said.

"It is already late," Jesus said. "These people have not had food all day. We cannot send them away. No, you give them food yourselves. Bring the fish and bread to Me. Then have the people sit down in groups of about fifty."

We did as He said. He took the fish and bread, gave thanks for them, and broke the loaves, putting the pieces in baskets. We went among the groups, passing out the baskets, and we could not believe our eyes! Everyone took as much food as they wanted from our baskets, and there seemed no end to the supply! When everyone had eaten, Jesus told us to gather up what was left, so that nothing would be wasted. When we did, we found that we had twelve baskets full of pieces!

Then Jesus sent us ahead of Him in the boat to the other side of the lake, saying He would join us there later.

We set out, rowing toward Capernaum. Soon it grew dark, and a storm arose. The wind blew against us. We strained at the oars, fighting the wind. Our boat foundered in the waves. *How could Jesus follow us now?* I wondered. One man in a boat would be helpless in this wind.

We had been at this for hours when suddenly someone pointed out across the stormy water. "A ghost!" he screamed. We looked, and our hearts froze!

There, off in the blackness of the night, we saw a figure in white coming toward us. It looked like a man. But there was no boat! We just stared, too terrified to move or speak. The figure came on. Now we could see that, yes, it was a man. He was walking as if along a street, right over the thrashing waves. He drew nearer and nearer. Suddenly someone shouted, "It is the Lord!"

"Courage!" came a familiar voice. "It is I." Now He was quite close. It did indeed look like Jesus. But was it really a ghost?

"Lord," I said, my voice shaking, "if it is really You, tell me to come to You."

"Come then, Simon," He said.

My heart pounding, I stepped onto the water, and stood! Now I began walking toward Jesus. Suddenly I realized what I was doing. I stopped. The wind howled around me. I looked down at my feet. Below me were the inky depths of the lake, the waves rolling under my feet. Terror seized me as I saw the water rising up over my feet, up my legs, past my waist. "Lord, save me!" I gasped, reaching out.

I felt His strong hand on my arm, pulling me up as if I were a doll. He led me to the boat. "Why did you doubt?" He asked.

Now we all bowed to Jesus. "Truly You are the Son of God!" we said.

CHAPTER 8

The crowds followed us even across the lake. That day, many people from Bethsaida came in boats and found us in Capernaum.

Jesus said, "You seek Me not because you saw miracles, but because you ate the fish and bread I gave you. Do not work for food that spoils but for the food that lasts for eternal life. This is the food the Son of Man will give you."

"What is the work that God requires of us?" they asked.

"That you believe in the One He sent," said Jesus.

"What sign, what miracle, can You give us so we can believe in You?" they asked. "Moses gave our ancestors manna, bread from heaven, to eat in the desert. What will You do?"

"Moses did not give you the bread from heaven," Jesus said. "My Father gives you the real bread from heaven. This bread gives life."

"Give us this bread!" they said.

"I am the Bread of Life," Jesus said. "He who comes to Me will never be hungry. If anyone eats this bread, he will live forever. The bread that I will give him is My flesh, which I give so that the world may live."

At this the people started arguing. "How can this man give us His flesh to eat?" some said.

Jesus said, "The words that I speak to you are spirit and life. Yet some of you do not believe. This is the reason I have said that no one can come to Me unless My Father makes it possible."

On hearing this, many of Jesus' followers turned back. Jesus turned to us twelve. "What about you?" He asked. "Do you wish to leave, too?"

"Lord," I said, "where would we go? You have the words of eternal life. And now we believe and know that You are the Holy One Who has come from God."

After this, we traveled only in the region of Galilee for awhile. We stayed out of Judea because the Jews there wanted to kill Jesus. In Galilee many people came to Jesus in the wilderness areas. He healed the sick and cast out many demons.

Now the Jewish Feast of the Tabernacles drew near. We went to Jerusalem for this feast, traveling mostly at night, so we could go about unseen. Jesus did not wish to be recognized until the day of the feast.

On the first day of the feast, Jesus entered the temple and began teaching. Immediately, the people recognized Him. The priests did not dare to arrest Jesus, because they were afraid of the people.

But even the people now seemed divided over Jesus. "Is He not the one the rulers are trying to kill?" some asked. "Look. Here He is, speaking openly, and they say nothing to Him! Have the rulers also come to believe that He is the Messiah?"

"How can He be the Messiah?" others said. "We know that when the Messiah comes, no one will know where He is from. Yet we know where this man is from."

Jesus said to them, "Do you know Me, and where I am from? You do not know the One Who sent Me, but I know Him, because I came from Him, and He sent Me."

Some in the crowd now shouted, "Seize Him! This is blasphemy!" But others said, "When the Messiah comes, will He do more than this man has done?" Still others said, "He is the Holy Prophet!" and, "He is the Messiah!" And the argument went on like this all day.

We left the temple, and Jesus went to the Mount of Olives, where He spent the night. Early the next morning He went back to the temple. People gathered to hear Him teach.

"I am the Light of the World," Jesus said. "Whoever follows Me will have the light of life and will never walk in darkness."

Some Pharisees now came up to Him. "You are testifying on Your own behalf," they said. "So Your testimony means nothing."

Jesus asked, "Is it not written in your Law that when two witnesses agree, what they say is true? I testify on My own behalf, and My Father testifies on My behalf."

"Where is Your Father?" they asked.

"If you knew Me, you would know My Father also," Jesus said.

"Our father is Abraham!" the Pharisees said.

"If Abraham really were your father, you would do the same things he did," said Jesus. "All I have ever done is tell you the truth, and for this you want to kill Me. Abraham did nothing like this! You are doing what your real father does."

"Our father is God Himself," they said.

"If God were your Father, you would love Me," Jesus said, "because I came from God. Why do you not understand what I say? It is because you cannot bear to listen to My message. You are the children of your father, the Devil, and you want to follow your father's desires. From the very beginning, he was a murderer and a liar. When he lies, it is from his own nature that he speaks, for he is the father of all lies. Yet because I tell you the truth, you do not believe Me. Anyone who is truly a child of God would believe My words. And My words are that whoever believes in Me will never die."

"You have a demon!" the Pharisees said. "Abraham himself died. Do You claim to be greater than he?"

"I make no claim to honor for Myself," Jesus said. "It is My Father who seeks to honor Me. But I tell you the truth; Abraham rejoiced that he was to see the time of My coming."

"You are not yet fifty years old!" they said. "And Abraham has seen You?"

"Before Abraham was born, I AM," Jesus said.

At this, the Pharisees tried to grab Him, but Jesus simply got up and walked out of the temple.

CHAPTER 9

After we left Jerusalem, we went far north, to the city of Caesarea Philippi. Our journey took many days. One morning on this journey, Jesus went off alone to pray. He often did this, many times staying away all night, but this day He soon returned. "Tell Me," He said, "Who do men say that I am?"

We answered, "Some say John the Baptist, others Elijah, and others Jeremiah or some other prophet."

"And you?" He said. "Who do you say I am?"

The words came out of my mouth before I really thought about them. "You are the Messiah," I said, "the Son of the living God."

Jesus said, "Blessed are you, Simon, son of John! For this truth did not come to you from any human being, but from My Father in heaven. So I tell you that you are 'Peter,' a rock, just as I am the Rock, the solid foundation on which everything of God was made. And on this Rock I will build My church. And against this church the gates of hell will not prevail! I will give you, Peter, the keys of the kingdom of heaven, and everything you bind or loose on earth will be bound or loosed in heaven."

As we walked, Jesus spoke plainly to us about what would happen to Him. "The Son of Man must suffer greatly," He said. "He will be rejected by the chief priests and the scribes, and He must be killed. But on the third day He will rise."

This thought shook me. How could it be? I learned only after Jesus' death what He had meant this day. But now I stopped Him on the road. "Lord!" I said, "this must never happen to You!"

Jesus looked straight into my eyes. He seemed to be staring past me, though, to something beyond me. "Get away from Me, Satan!" He said. "This is not God's thought, but man's. You are an obstacle in the path My Father has chosen for Me!"

Then Jesus said, "If anyone wants to come after Me, he must forget himself, carry his cross daily, and follow Me. Whoever seeks to save his own life will lose it, but whoever loses his life for My sake will find it. For what will a person gain who wins the whole world but loses his life?"

It was six days after this that I saw Jesus' glory revealed. I will never forget the sight! One morning He woke me and asked me to go with Him up a tall mountain nearby. He also called the brothers James and John. We climbed to the top in the growing daylight.

At the top we all knelt down and prayed. Or at least Jesus prayed. I did not really know how to pray yet. Soon Jesus went off by Himself. As we watched Him kneeling, suddenly He seemed to burst into flames. His face and clothes were whiter than anything I had ever seen. And now as we stared, two other men suddenly appeared. They, too, were clothed in brightness. Jesus talked with these two.

Somehow I knew who these men were, even though no one told me. I was so shaken that I did not know what to do or say. "Lord," I stammered, "it is good that we disciples are here. We will make three shelters, one for You, one for Moses, and one for Elijah."

But just as I said this, a great light appeared overhead. We looked up and saw a cloud as white as Jesus and the two men. And a voice came from the cloud, saying, "This is My own dear Son, with Whom I am pleased. Listen to Him!"

James, John, and I fell to our faces on the ground, trembling. "Get up," came Jesus' voice. "Do not be afraid." We looked up. Jesus was alone. The other men and the cloud were gone. "Do not tell anyone what you have seen here," Jesus said, "until the Son of Man has been raised from death."

The crowds still came to us and followed Jesus, but there were fewer people now, and many of them began asking Jesus to prove Himself. "Show us a sign," they would say.

This grieved Jesus. "The only sign you will be given is the sign of Jonah," He said. "Just as Jonah spent three days in the belly of a fish, so shall the Son of Man spend three days in the depths of the earth, to be raised to life on the third day."

Jesus began spending more time alone with us disciples. He taught us about the kingdom of God, explaining things to us in plain words.

One day as we walked in the streets of Capernaum, we disciples were arguing about who among us was the greatest. Jesus came up to us. "Sit down, all of you," He said. We sat by the side of the street, and Jesus sat with us. "Why were you arguing about who is the greatest?" He asked. We were too ashamed to answer.

"If anyone wishes to be first, he must be last of all," Jesus said. Then He called a little girl who was walking by. She came to Him shyly. Tenderly He took her in His arms. I had never seen my Lord's face so full of love. His eyes shone.

"Whoever humbles himself as this little child here will be great in heaven," He said. "I tell you, unless you become like little children, you will never enter the kingdom of heaven. And whoever receives a child like this in My name also receives not only Me but My Father.

"What do you think a man does who has a hundred sheep and loses one?" Jesus continued. "He will leave the others and look for the lost sheep. When he finds it, he is far happier with it than with the ninety-nine that were not lost. In the same way, your Father in heaven does not want any of these little ones to be lost."

Soon after this, in the city of Bethany, we were invited to the home of two sisters, Martha and Mary. All day Mary sat with Jesus, asking Him questions and listening to His words.

Toward evening, Martha came to Jesus. She was angry. "Lord, do You not care that my sister has left me to do all the preparation?" she asked. "Tell her to come and help me!"

Jesus took Martha by the hand. "Martha, Martha," He said, "you are troubled about many things. But only one thing is needed, and Mary has chosen the best thing. This cannot be taken away from her."

During these days, many Pharisees came in groups to see Jesus. They tried to trap Him with questions, hoping He would say something against their Law. They wished for nothing more than to have Him arrested and killed. Many, many people had put their faith in Jesus. These people saw the truth about how the Pharisees lied and cheated for their own gain, how they used religion simply to satisfy their selfish desires. And Jesus had hard words for the Pharisees.

"You Pharisees clean the outside of your cup," He said, "but inside you are full of violence and evil. Fools! Did not God, who made the outside, also make the inside?

"How terrible for you Pharisees! You give God a tenth of your seasonings and herbs, but you neglect justice and love for God.

"How terrible for you Pharisees! You love the best seats in the synagogues and to be greeted with respect in the marketplaces. You are like whitewashed tombs. Outside you look clean, but inside you are full of bones and filth.

"How terrible for you teachers! You put heavy loads on the back of the people to whom you teach the Law. But you yourselves will not even lift a finger to help these people carry those loads. You teachers have kept the key that opens the door to knowledge. But you yourselves will not enter, and you stop those who are trying to enter."

Jesus was criticized bitterly for saying these things, but the Pharisees and teachers never trapped Him with their questions. Eventually, no one dared ask Him any more questions. In His answers, He spoke only the truth, and His accusers could not bear the truth.

CHAPTER 10

We began to make our way slowly toward Jerusalem, going through all the cities and villages along the way. It would be the last time Jesus ever entered Jerusalem, He told us. He told us again how the Son of Man would be handed over to the rulers and would be tortured and killed.

In the cities and villages, Jesus continued to heal all who came to Him and to teach the crowds that gathered. He did not go into the synagogues now, though. All the leaders of the Jewish religion were against Him. So people came to Him in the streets, in the village squares, on the roads between cities, and even in the wilderness.

One day, we sat outside a village among a group of people. A man asked Jesus, "Lord, will only a few be saved?"

Jesus said, "Try to enter the narrow door, because many will try but will not be able. The master of the house will shut the door, and you will knock outside saying, 'Lord, Lord, open the door for us.' He will answer, 'I do not know you.' And you will say, 'We ate bread with you. You taught in the streets of our city.' But he will answer, 'I do not know where you come from. Get away from me, you wicked people!' People will come from the east and west, from the north and south, and sit down at the feast in the kingdom of

God. Then those who are now last will be first, and those who are now first will be last."

One evening I went with Jesus to a Pharisee's home. We had been invited there to dinner. As we ate, Jesus spoke to the other guests.

"When you give a banquet, do not invite your friends or relatives," He said. "They can invite you in return and pay you back. Instead, invite the poor, the lame, and the blind, because they cannot pay you back. You will be paid for the good things you do on the day of resurrection."

One of the guests then said, "How happy are those who will sit down at the feast in the kingdom of God!"

Jesus said, "There was once a man who was giving a great feast to which he had invited many people. When it was time for the feast, he sent his servants to bring his guests, but his guests began making excuses for not coming. One by one, they refused the invitation. The servants went back and told their master that no one would come. The master said to the servants, 'Hurry into the streets and bring back the poor, the crippled, the blind. And go to the country roads and invite everyone in, so my house will be full. But I tell you that none of those who were first invited will taste my dinner!'

Soon after this, we were walking on a road in Samaria when we were met by ten men with leprosy, a terrible skin disease. They recognized Jesus. "Jesus, Master, have mercy on us!" they cried.

Jesus said, "Go to the priest and have him examine you, according to the Law."

They quickly went down the road. Shortly after, one of them came running up to us again. He knelt in the road at Jesus' feet and thanked Him. Then he stood up. His skin had been blotchy and discolored, but now it was clear and healthy.

"There were ten of you," Jesus said. "And yet you, not a Jew but a Samaritan, are the only one who gives thanks to God. Go on your way. Your faith has made you well."

We had not gone far when a young man came running up to us. "I am a messenger from Bethany," he panted. "I am sent by the sisters Mary and Martha. Their brother Lazarus is sick and dying. They wish You to come."

Now we knew that Jesus loved the sisters and their brother. We expected Him to be alarmed at hearing that Lazarus was dying, but He calmly said, "This sickness will not end in death, but for the glory of God." And He told the messenger, "I will come when I can."

We then went into the nearest village. "Lord," I said, "do You not care that Your friend Lazarus is dying?"

He did not answer. We disciples wondered what had come over Jesus. We tarried in that village for two days. On the third day, Jesus said we would go to Bethany. "Our friend Lazarus has fallen asleep," He said. "Now I will go waken him."

The journey to Bethany took two days. Before we entered the city, Martha met us on the road, weeping bitterly. "Lord," she said, "if You had been here, my brother would not have died!'

Jesus said, "Your brother will rise to life."

"I know that he will, on the last day," she said.

"I am the resurrection and the life," Jesus said. "Whoever believes in Me will live, even though he dies. And whoever lives and believes in Me will never die. Do you believe this, Martha?"

"Yes," she said. "I do believe that You are the Messiah!"

Many people were at Martha's house to comfort her and Mary. Some were from Jerusalem, which was less than two miles from Bethany. When Jesus saw Mary and all her friends lost in grief, He was so filled with compassion that He wept. "See how much He loves his friend Lazarus!" someone said.

Then Jesus said to Mary, "Show Me your brother's tomb." We went outside the city to a small hill. In the side of the hill was a large stone that covered a hole.

"Take the stone away!" Jesus said.

"But, Lord!" said Martha, horrified, "he has been dead for four days. The smell will be terrible!"

"Did I not tell you that you would see God's glory if you believe?" asked Jesus. Then He said to some men standing near, "Take the stone away." They obeyed silently.

No one spoke. No one even moved. What was Jesus going to do? A look of horror and fear was on everyone's face. The stone was moved. A black pit gaped in the hillside. My temples throbbed. Jesus raised His hand. My heart jumped. "Lazarus, come forth!" Jesus said, in a voice that seemed to shake the earth.

Everyone gasped. From out of that dark hole, that tomb, came a man wrapped in the clothes of the dead!

"Praise the name of the Lord!" came the shouts. "The Son of God has come!" News of this spread quickly to Jerusalem.

CHAPTER 11

We did not know it then, but we learned later that some of the Jews from Jerusalem who had been at Lazarus's tomb went to the priests in Jerusalem and told them what Jesus had done. This made the priests more determined than ever to kill Jesus. They met in secret council. "If we let this man go on performing miracles like this, all Rome will hear of it," they said. "The Romans will come and take over our beloved temples and destroy our very religion. We will lose all our power over the people." And they began plotting a way to kill Jesus.

Somehow Jesus knew of this. He seemed to know a lot of things before they happened. Many times, He could tell what a person was thinking. Now we did not go among the Jews but stayed more and more in the wilderness. Soon we went north to a town called Ephraim, where we stayed for a couple of days before starting for Jerusalem.

On our way, we passed through the city of Jericho. There a man met us in the street. He wore an expensive robe and gold rings on his fingers. He recognized Jesus. "Good teacher," he said, "what must I do to inherit eternal life?"

"Why do you call Me good?" Jesus asked. "There is only One Who is good—your Father in heaven. But if you wish to have eternal life, you must obey the commandments. Do not murder, steal, lie, cheat, or commit adultery. Honor your parents, and love your neighbors as yourself."

"I have done these things all my life," said the man.

Jesus looked at him with love. "You lack one thing," He said. "Go sell all that you own, give the money to the poor, and then come and follow Me."

The man's face fell. He turned and walked away with his head down. Jesus looked after him sadly. Then He said to us, "How hard it will be for the rich to enter heaven! I tell you, it is easier for a camel to pass through the eye of a sewing needle than for a rich man to enter the kingdom of God. Such a man loves his riches more than God."

As we went on, Jesus told again of His coming death. "We are going to Jerusalem," He said.

"There everything written by the prophets about the Son of Man will come true. The chief priests will condemn Him to death. He will be tortured and mocked and spit on. They will whip Him and kill Him. But on the third day He will rise."

We did not understand why Jesus said this or why it should have to happen as He said, but as we went, a sense of doom seemed to cover us. It hung on us heavily.

A crowd had gathered around us in the street. More and more people joined us. Suddenly Jesus stopped and looked up into a fig tree. A man was sitting in the branches.

"Zacchaeus, come down," Jesus said. "I am going to your house today."

The man scrambled down and pushed his way through the crowd. His face was eager, like a child's. But many in the crowd began to scorn him and Jesus. "This man is a tax collector and a cheat," they cried. "How is it that You go to his home and treat him as a friend?"

Jesus shook His head. "I have not come to call the saved, but the lost," He said. "People who are well do not need a doctor but only those who are sick."

Now Zacchaeus, who was very small, led Jesus and us to his house. There he waited on us, bustling about busily. He was awed and overjoyed in the presence of Jesus. "Lord," he said, "I will give half my possessions to the poor." Tears came to his eyes. "And if I have cheated anyone, I will restore his property four times over."

Jesus smiled at him. "Today salvation has come to this house," He said, "to you and all your family."

The days of the Passover celebration were again drawing near, so we set out for Jerusalem. Six days before the Passover, we came to Bethany, where we stayed that night with Lazarus and his sisters.

The next day we started again for Jerusalem. We came to a small village called Bethphage. Before we entered, Jesus sent two of us ahead into the village. "As soon as you enter the village, you will find a donkey tied up," He said. "Untie it and bring it to Me. If anyone asks you what you are doing, say, 'The Master has sent for this.' "

These two did as Jesus said. Soon they returned with the donkey. Their faces showed awe. "Master!" they said, 'it was just as You said it would be!"

Jesus rode this donkey into Jerusalem. Many people were in the city for the Passover. As Jesus entered, crowds flocked to us. "Blessed is the King who comes in the name of the Lord!" they shouted. "Hosanna to the Son of David! Hosanna to the King of Israel!" And the people cut branches from palm trees and spread these and their cloaks on the ground before Jesus.

We came like this to the temple. The whole city seemed in an uproar. People everywhere were shouting and praising God.

We entered the temple, and the crowds followed, singing and shouting. The priests looked furious, but they could say nothing. People poured in from the streets. Jesus healed everyone who came to Him. Children danced and sang praises to God. "Praise to David's Son! Praise to God!" And the priests gathered in the shadows of the temple and whispered together.

The next morning when we entered the temple, only a few people were there. Now the chief priests came up to Jesus. "Who gave You the right to do these things?" they asked.

"If you can answer one question, I will tell you," Jesus said. "Where did John the Baptist's authority come from, God or man?"

The priests looked at one another in surprise. Now they began arguing. One said, "If we answer, 'From God,' He will say, 'Why did you not listen to him?' But if we say, 'From man,' there might be rioting in the temple, because the people here all believe John was from God." So they answered, "We do not know."

Jesus said, "Neither will I tell you, then, where My authority comes from."

Now Jesus asked the priests another question. "Tell Me," He said, "what do you think? A man had two sons. To one, he said, 'Go and work in the vineyard today.' The son said, 'I will not,' but later repented and went. To the other son, the man said, 'You, too, go work in the vineyard.' The son said, 'Yes, Sir,' but did not go. Now, which of these sons did the will of his father?"

"The first," said the priests.

"So I tell you," said Jesus, "that tax collectors and harlots are going into the kingdom of God ahead of you. For John the Baptist came to you, showing you the path to take, and you would not believe him. But the tax collectors and harlots did. Even when you saw this, you did not change your minds and believe him.

"Listen to another parable," Jesus continued. "Once a

landowner planted a vineyard, which he rented to tenants before he left on a trip. When harvesttime came, he sent his slaves to the tenants for his share of the harvest, but the tenants beat the slaves, killing one, and sent the rest back empty-handed. The owner sent more slaves, who were treated the same way. Finally, he sent his only son. 'Surely they must respect my son,' he thought. But the tenants grabbed the son, beat him, and killed him. Now, when the owner of this vineyard comes, what will he do to those people?"

"He will surely kill those evil men and rent the vineyards to others," said the priests.

Jesus said, "Haven't you read this Scripture? 'The stone that the builders rejected as worthless turned out to be the most important of all'? And so I tell you that the kingdom of God will be taken away from you and given to a people who will produce the proper fruit."

The priests would have arrested Jesus right then, but they were afraid of the people gathering in the temple.

Later, as Jesus was teaching the crowds in the temple, a Pharisee came alone to Him. He did not seem to be trying to trap Jesus by questions. Rather, he seemed to be hungering for the truth. "Teacher," he said, "which commandment in the Law is the greatest one?"

Jesus said, "The most important is this. 'Listen, Israel! The Lord our God is the only Lord. Love the Lord your God with all your heart, with all your soul, with all your mind, and with all your strength.' The second most important commandment is this. 'Love your neighbor as you love yourself.' There is no other commandment more important than these two."

The Pharisee said, "Well spoken, Teacher! It is true, as You say, that only the Lord is God, and that there is no other God but He. And man must love God and his neighbor, just as you say. It is more important to obey these two commandments than to offer animals and other sacrifices on the altar to God."

"You have spoken wisely, My friend," said Jesus. "You are not far yourself from the kingdom of God."

Then Jesus said, in a voice that silenced the whole crowd, "Whoever believes in Me believes not only in Me but also in Him who sent Me. I have come into the world as Light, so that everyone who believes in Me should not remain in darkness. If anyone hears My message and does not obey it, I will not judge him. I came not to judge the world but to save it. Whoever rejects Me has One who will judge him. The words I have spoken will be his judge on the last day."

CHAPTER 12

It was now the day of unleavened bread, when the Passover meal was to be prepared. Jesus told us how we were to find a room where we would eat the Passover meal, and it was just as He said. We prepared the lamb, the unleavened bread, and the herbs and spices. When all was ready, Jesus and the rest of the disciples came. We were in a small upper-story room in the heart of Jerusalem.

"I have yearned to eat this meal with you before I must suffer," Jesus said. "I will not eat it again until it is fulfilled in the kingdom of God."

While we were eating, Jesus took off His robe and poured a large bowl of water. Then He got down on His knees and went around the table to each of us. And the Lord, the Son of God, washed our feet and dried them with a towel. "What I am doing you do not understand," He said, "but you will understand later."

When He had finished, He put on his robe and sat with us again. "You call Me Lord," He said, "and in this you speak the truth, for that is Who I am. Yet I, the Lord, have washed your feet. The Son of Man did not come as 'lord' to be served, as your earthly kings are. But He came to serve. This is how you, too, must serve one another.

"I say this not to all of you, though," Jesus continued. "One of you will betray Me!"

We were startled. "Lord, who is he?" we asked.

"It is one of you twelve, who now eat with Me, whom I give this bread to," He said. He broke a piece of bread and handed it to Judas Iscariot. "Do quickly what you are about to do," He said to Judas. And Judas hurried out of the room. We did not understand this. We thought Jesus had sent Judas on some errand. Only later did we learn that Judas had secretly gone to the chief priests at the temple and offered to betray Jesus. The priests had agreed to pay Judas for his treachery.

After Judas left, Jesus took His wine cup, filled it, and broke a chunk of bread. He handed the bread to each of us. "Take this," he said. "Eat. This is My body, which is broken for you. Do this in memory of Me." Then He passed the wine to each of us. "Drink this," He said. "This is My blood, which is poured out for you. This is the blood of a new covenant I am making with you. With My blood I am washing your sins clean.

"And I give you a new command," He said. "You must love one another, just as I have loved you. All the world will know My disciples by their love toward one another. I am going away soon. I am returning to the Father, from Whom I came. But I will send the Spirit to you when I am gone. He will come so you will not be alone. And My peace I leave with you. You will be filled with My peace."

"Lord," I said, "I am ready to follow You now."

"Peter, I tell you the truth," Jesus said. "Before the rooster crows, you will deny Me three times."

"Never, Lord!" I said. The tears streamed down my face. There were sorrow and love in my Lord's eyes. "I will never deny You!" I said. "Not even if I have to die with You!" And the other disciples swore the same thing.

"My Father's house has many rooms," Jesus said. "I am going to prepare a place for each of you. And you will know where I am going, and you will know the way."

Thomas said, "Lord, we do not know where You are going or the way."

Jesus said, "I am the Way, the Truth, and the Life. No one comes to the Father but through Me. If you had known Me, you would have known my Father also. And from now on you do know Him and have seen Him."

Philip said, "Show us the Father! That is all we need."

"For a long time I have been with you," Jesus said. "And yet you still do not know Me, Philip? Whoever has seen Me has seen the Father. Do you not know, Philip, that I am in the Father and the Father is in Me? This is the truth. The Father and I are one. And whoever believes in Me will do what I do—even greater things than I have done. If you remain in Me, and My word remains in you, then you will ask for anything you wish, and you shall have it."

Later that night, after we had sung hymns to God, we went with Jesus out of the city. We went across Kidron Brook to a garden called Gethsemane.

Jesus' face was full of something like agony. "Stay here," He said. "I am going to pray." He went off a little way by Himself.

The night was very dark and still. The stars shimmered in a clear sky. A fresh, earthy smell filled the garden. It should have been a place of beauty, of childlike wonder perhaps. But that night, to me, the stars glittered like the blades of deadly knives, the earthy smell of the garden was as suffocating as a grave, and the very darkness of the night hid terrors, crouching, waiting. Something was wrong in the universe. Deathly wrong.

Jesus' voice came to us. There was an agony in it I had never heard from Him, or from any man. "Father," He said, "if it is possible, let Me not drink of this cup!" Then He came back to us. And His face! What pain I saw there! Sweat poured from Him like blood.

"The sorrow in My heart is so great it crushes Me," He said. "Stay here and keep watch with Me while I pray." He went off again. Listening to His voice, I fell asleep.

"Could you not even stay awake with Me for one hour?" The voice woke me. Jesus stood in front of us. The other disciples had also fallen asleep and were now waking. A pale light shone in the east.

"But now, look," Jesus said. In the growing light of morning, we saw a large group of men coming toward us. "The hour has come!"

CHAPTER 13

Now we could see the priests of the temple with many soldiers, led by Judas Iscariot, who came up to Jesus and kissed Him. "Hail, Master," Judas said.

"So, Judas," said Jesus, "you betray the Son of Man with a kiss."

The soldiers grabbed Jesus. We later learned that Judas had said, "The one I greet is the one you want."

Now fury rose up in me. I drew my sword and struck at the nearest man, the bondservant of the high priest. My blow cut off his right ear.

"Stop!" said Jesus. "Do you not know, Peter, that if I wished, I could call an army of angels here now, and they would come? This is only happening as it must happen. I am permitting all this." He touched the man's bleeding face and healed him.

Now panic overcame us disciples. We fled, not knowing where to run, or why. But I soon stopped running. Where were they taking my Lord? What would happen to Him? I followed the group from a distance.

Jesus was led to an inner courtyard of the temple. There the priests hurled accusations at Him. I stopped in an outer courtyard. The morning was cold, and the soldiers had lit a fire. I stood there among the people, warming my hands.

Suddenly someone said, "You are one of His disciples!"

I was terrified. I stammered, "No, I am not."

Soon another man looked at me and said, "You are one of them." Again I denied it.

Again someone saw me and said, "You were with this man, were you not?" And for the third time, I denied it.

Just then I heard a rooster crow. And then I remembered: "Before the rooster crows, you will deny Me three times."

Like a walking dead man, I turned and went out of the temple. As I walked, I began to weep, and my anguish poured from me like blood from my heart. I had denied my Lord, my Savior, my beloved Friend! I do not know how long I walked. My heart was cold; my world destroyed. What happened next was a nightmare.

It was the next day. Jesus was in the palace of the governor, Pontius Pilate. Jesus was dressed in a purple robe. A crown of thorns was embedded in His head. Blood seeped from His back through His robe. Soldiers surrounded Him. They spit on Him and punched Him. They cawed and jeered. "Hail to the King of the Jews!" they mocked. Jesus staggered under their blows and winced as they spit in His face. Yet His arms hung at His sides, and His shoulders were stooped.

Then it was the day after that. Jesus stood by Pilate, who was seated on a platform facing a vast crowd of people, most of them Jews. Some in the crowd were weeping, but many more were shouting in fury, "Crucify Him! Crucify Him!"

The governor stood up. He seemed troubled. "But He has done nothing to deserve death!" he said.

The crowd screamed all the louder. "Crucify Him!"

"Shall I crucify your King?" cried Pilate.

"We have no king but Caesar!" they shouted.

"But what crime has He committed?"

"Crucify Him! Crucify Him!"

Pilate slumped to his chair. He said in a weak voice, "I am innocent of this man's blood."

"His blood will be on our heads, and on our children's heads!" screamed the Jews among the crowd. And the cry of "Crucify Him!" grew in pitch and became a chant. Jesus was led away.

He was whipped again, with leather lashes in which were tied sharp pieces of bone. The bone pieces ripped out chunks of flesh from His back, chest, and shoulders. Those flogging Him seemed possessed. They lashed at Jesus in uncontrollable fury.

When He came out of the city, He was slick with His own blood. It covered Him from head to foot. The memory of His words, "My blood is shed for you," cut through me like a sword.

Across Jesus' shoulders, tied to His outspread arms, lay a heavy wooden beam, the transept of a cross. He staggered under its weight. Many times He fell. Without His arms to catch Himself, He fell on His face, which soon was battered to a pulp. He left a blood-spattered trail behind Him as He labored on. The crowd hooted and jeered. No one helped Him up when He fell. Sometimes it seemed like hours before He could get to His feet again.

He came like this to a hill called Golgotha, the Skull. Here He fell and could not rise. Now soldiers threw Him onto the upright of the cross. They drove long spikes through His wrists and ankles into the hard wood. Then they lifted the cross and dropped it into place.

Over Jesus' head was an inscription that Pilate had ordered carved: "This is Jesus of Nazareth, King of the Jews."

And on that day, on that hill, evil was a living, crawling thing. It writhed through the crowd like a snake. People screamed insults at the bloody figure on the cross. "Save Yourself! Come down from the cross, and we will believe in You!" And at the foot of the cross, the soldiers cast lots on the ground, gambling for Jesus' linen robe, which lay on the ground.

At midday, suddenly the sky became dark as night. The looks of wild hatred froze on the faces of those nearest the cross. No one moved. No one spoke. I heard only my heart beating.

The darkness hung over the whole land for three hours. Then Jesus cried out in a blood-choked voice, "My God,

My God, why have You abandoned Me?" His breath came in shallow, ragged gasps. He was drowning in blood from His battered chest. I could hear His voice burbling faintly, "Father, forgive them, for they do not know what they are doing." Then His head slumped forward. He was dead.

Then the earth came alive. The ground shuddered under our feet. The shudder became a rumble, and the rumble became a roar. All the earth shook, as if in fury. Great boulders on the hillsides cracked and split apart and tumbled downhill.

The crowd scattered in every direction. Tough soldiers wailed like babies in their terror. People beat their breasts and pulled their hair as they reeled over the trembling ground.

And from within the heart of the temple came a shrieking, rending sound. The massive tapestried curtain to the Holy of Holies was ripped like paper from top to bottom. The two ragged pieces hung like corpses.

Three days later, the eleven of us found one another and met in the room where we had eaten the Passover meal with our Lord. We nursed our grief together late into the evening.

We had come to believe in Him as the Messiah, the Promised One. And then He was murdered on a cross!

Our door was locked that night. We had reason to hide. The priests hated us as His disciples. We talked about what to do, where to go now.

Suddenly a figure entered the room, right through the locked door! We gasped.

"Peace to you," said a familiar voice. Jesus!

"A ghost!" we screamed.

The figure walked up to us. "Does a ghost have flesh and bone?" He said. "Touch Me. Do you not remember that I told you I would rise on the third day?"

In awe, we each touched His hands, His face. There were jagged scars on His wrists. He was the same, yet different. He was stronger, brighter, as if death had tempered Him like steel in fire.

We were overcome by joy! We knelt and worshiped Him. "My Lord and my God!" we cried.

He stayed with us many hours that night, and He came to us several times after that. On the day He left us, He reminded us that He would return in Spirit. "Go now into all the world and make everyone My disciple," He said. "And I will be with you always, until the end of all things."

It was not the end, but only the beginning.

THE MIRACLES OF JESUS

by Ellyn Sanna

CHAPTER 1

"Come on," Aaron called over his shoulder. "Grandfather John promised to tell me one of his stories. You can listen, too."

Eleven-year-old Rachel hung back, frowning. Aaron was her new friend—her only friend here in Ephesus—and she liked being with him. But listening to an old man talk didn't sound very interesting to her. Besides, she was hungry. She had planned on heading for the market, hoping that someone would have bruised figs they would be willing to give her. And maybe she could even get hold of a bone for soup. That would make her mother happy. . . .

Ever since her father died two years ago, Rachel was nearly always hungry. Her mother did the best she could to find them food, but they had no relatives to help support them, and they grew poorer and poorer. They had moved from Corinth to Ephesus last spring, hoping things would be better, but their house here was little more than a few boards nailed together.

Rachel's eyes burned as she thought about their troubles. *It's not fair,* she thought fiercely. They hadn't done anything to deserve such a cold, hungry, sad life. She was tired of always thinking about food; she was tired of her mother always being sad and weary; and most of all she was tired of always missing her father. . . .

Aaron broke into her thoughts. "Come on," he insisted. He walked backward down the street, grinning at her. "You'll like Grandfather John. I promise."

Rachel made a face. But when Aaron ducked through an arched opening in the wall beside the street, she sighed and followed him through into an inner courtyard.

They found an old man sitting on a stone bench, the sun shining on his snow-white hair. He turned his lined face toward the two children and smiled. "Aaron." His dark eyes were bright with welcome. "And who is your friend?" His gaze moved to Rachel's face with gentle curiosity.

Self-consciously, Rachel tucked her hair behind her ears and smoothed her ragged robe, suddenly aware that her face and hands were dusty, and her hair was snarled and rough. Lately, her mother had no time to notice if Rachel was clean or not—and somehow Rachel always forgot to check until it was too late.

"This is Rachel. She's new in Ephesus." Aaron flung himself down on the dirt at the old man's feet. "Her mother is a widow," he added bluntly.

Rachel felt herself flush, and she wished she and Aaron were alone so she could smack him on the head. She scowled down at her dirty toes. "I should go," she muttered.

The old man put out a thin, wrinkled hand. "No, stay.

Please." He met Rachel's eyes and smiled. "My grandson loves to hear stories about the Master. You're welcome to listen, too."

Rachel bit her lip, uncertain whether to go or stay. She had chores to do before her mother came back from "gleaning"—picking up the unwanted loose grain from the farmers' fields outside the city wall. Rachel was still hoping to get something from the market, something to ease the emptiness in her own stomach and a bit more to surprise her mother. But the sun was still high in the sky, and she supposed she could be hungry a little longer. Something about the old man's face made her want to stay, even if she had to listen to boring stories about long ago. She plopped down in the dust beside Aaron and asked, "Who is the Master?"

Aaron nudged her with his elbow. "You know—the Messiah. Jesus the Christ. You've heard my parents call Him the Master."

Rachel shrugged. She usually didn't pay much attention to what grown-ups said, except when they gave her food. Since her father died, Rachel was too busy figuring out how to help her mother get their next meal. Aaron's mother often gave Rachel baskets of bread and cheese, and Rachel was always both grateful and embarrassed. But she had never noticed Aaron's mother talking about any "Master."

Aaron was staring at her, his eyebrows raised. "You do know Who Jesus is, don't you?"

Rachel shrugged again. She seemed to remember her father once saying something about Jesus of Nazareth. . . and maybe she'd heard some gossip in the marketplace, back when they lived in Corinth. "Wasn't He a magician or something?" The look on Aaron's face made her search her mind for something more. "He was crucified, wasn't He?" She turned away from Aaron's disgusted expression and looked up at the old man.

John nodded gravely. "Yes, He was crucified. But He was more than a magician. He was the Son of God. He was God, come down to be with us."

Rachel tucked in the corner of her mouth. The old man didn't look crazy, but still. . . "How do you know?" she asked flatly.

Aaron pushed his sandal against Rachel's ankle. "Grandfather John was one of the Master's twelve disciples," he told her between his teeth. Aaron was clearly not pleased with Rachel's ignorance. "He spent three years with Jesus. He knew Him better than anyone. They were friends."

Show some respect, Aaron's brown eyes told Rachel silently. She looked away from his gaze, back to the old man. He smiled at her, apparently undisturbed, and put a quieting hand on his grandson's shoulder.

"Jesus proved to us Who He was by signs and miracles," he told Rachel gently.

"So He was a magician," Rachel said stubbornly. "Like

I said." She searched her memory for the gossip she had heard about this man. "Didn't He claim to be able to turn water into wine, stuff like that?"

John nodded. "He did turn water into wine once, at a wedding in Cana. But His miracles were not just tricks meant to entertain. His miracles told us about God. They showed us the kingdom of heaven."

Rachel wrinkled her nose. "Heaven?" she repeated, not sure what the old man meant. "You mean like when we die?"

"M–m–m." John squinted up at the sky and shook his head. "All this—" He waved his hand around the courtyard, taking in the small square house and the city street beyond the wall. "Ephesus, the lands beyond; they are all part of the Roman emperor's kingdom. Once we Jews lived in the kingdom ruled by David's throne, and we long for the day when our land will be our own again. But David and the Roman emperors both ruled earthly kingdoms, kingdoms we can see and touch."

He smiled up at the blue sky above his head, and his voice became softer, filled with a strange joy that Rachel did not understand. "But there is another kingdom all around us, an invisible kingdom, the kingdom of heaven. Jesus is the Lord of this realm—and through faith in Him, the things we can see and touch become part of heaven's kingdom. We who follow the Master believe that through faith we are now citizens of heaven. And our Lord's miracles showed us that He controls our world, that He has the power to bring everything under His rule. His miracles showed us Who God is—and they showed us what His kingdom is like."

Rachel's eyes followed the old man's gaze to the blue sky. Her stomach growled loudly, distracting her for a moment, but in spite of herself, she was interested in this invisible kingdom. She wondered if people still got hungry once they were citizens of heaven. Then she shook her head at her own thoughts, and her eyes dropped back to the dusty earth beneath her. "It still sounds like magic to me," she said.

"No," John said gently. "It is not magic. Jesus had amazing power, it is true, but He did not use His power to impress people or for His own purposes. His miracles tell us good news—that God's love is with us. God's kingdom is real, even more real than the world we see around us."

Rachel was silent while her mind pondered these new ideas. Beside her, Aaron sat quietly, his chin on his drawn-up knees. She glanced at him, glad he was no longer impatient with her, and then she turned back to John once more. "And you actually saw this Jesus perform these miracles? They weren't tricks?"

"I saw them," John affirmed. "They weren't tricks."

Rachel studied his face, wondering if he spoke the truth. Somehow, his words made her prickle inside. She felt something strange, something different than she had felt since her father died. It felt like. . .hope.

She sniffed. What use would an invisible kingdom be to her mother and her? *It won't feed us,* she reminded herself.

"So tell me about these miracles," she said to the old man. She knew her voice was louder than it should be. *Talk like a woman,* her mother was always reminding her. *Speak softly, with your eyes lowered. You are rude when you look older people full in the face and talk with that sharp little voice of yours.* But speaking softly made Rachel feel angry. Besides, no one noticed a grimy, ragged little girl if she didn't look straight at them and make them see her. Rachel lifted her chin a notch, daring the old man to disapprove of her. "What was the greatest miracle Jesus ever did?"

The old man smiled at her with such a look of acceptance and love that Rachel blinked. He sat back on the stone bench more comfortably, and then he closed his eyes and tilted his face toward the sun's warmth. Rachel thought he was going to sleep, but then he said slowly, "I suppose the greatest miracle of the Master's life would have to be the one that started them all."

"You mean the time He turned the water into wine?" Aaron asked.

His grandfather shook his head. "No. That miracle and all the others were caused by this first great miracle—and they all proved that it was true." He fell silent.

"So what was it?" Rachel asked impatiently.

John opened his eyes. "Why, His birth."

CHAPTER 2

"In the beginning, before anything else existed," John began, "Jesus was already alive. We can't imagine what that must have been like, because we can't imagine anything beyond what we have always known. But there in the darkness, before the sun and the stars began to burn, was God, and Jesus was with Him. Jesus wasn't just with God, though. He actually was God. God the Creator and Jesus and the Holy Spirit are all separate and yet One, the way the three strands of a rope twist together to make one cord.

"Jesus was there when the earth was formed, and the water, and the sky, and all the living things on the earth. His power was at work while all these things were being made, because nothing exists anywhere that He didn't make. He made life, because He is where all life begins. This life gives light to us all today, and it has lit the lives of the generations of people who have lived upon the earth since our father, Adam, and our mother, Eve. Jesus continues to give light and life forever, because nothing can ever blow out His light. In the darkness, before Creation, it shone as brightly as it does now, and it shines the same even in the midst of sadness and hurt and evil. Death itself cannot cast a shadow over the light of Christ.

"And this same Jesus, this ageless, undying being, loves us. Before the world was made, He loved you and me. He loved us so much that He did something amazing, something truly miraculous. He became a human baby and was born to a virgin named Mary.

"Can you imagine what that means? The Creator of the universe loved us so much that He emptied Himself of all His power. As the Son of God, He could be everywhere at the same time. He could do anything at all, so awesome was His power. And He knew everything, all the secrets of the universe. But He gave up all that and became a tiny, helpless little baby.

"Before He was born, the angels told His parents, Mary and Joseph, what was going to happen. And on the night He was born, heaven's choir sang to some poor shepherds who were watching their sheep out on the hills. A few other people were told of this marvelous thing that was happening.

"But for the most part, Jesus arrived on earth very quietly. He grew up in Nazareth, the Son of God now a simple carpenter. But those who knew Him then already noticed something different about Him. He was so full of love. Everything about Him reached out to others.

"Most of us, you know, even children, walk around with walls around our hearts. But Jesus didn't have any walls. He gave Himself to everyone He met. And He didn't try to protect Himself with lies and fancy acts to impress others. No,

He always told the truth. His life was the truth.

"Now God sent another man, Jesus' cousin, John the Baptist, to tell people that God's Son was coming to change their hearts. John the Baptist was like a big signpost pointing toward Jesus. 'Change the way you live!' John shouted. 'Stop being so selfish! Start loving each other! Start sharing with each other! Someone is coming Who is far greater than I am, for He existed long before I did.'

"But even though John did what he could to get people ready for the Messiah, a lot of people still did not recognize Jesus when they saw Him. They had a picture in their heads of what the Messiah ought to act like—they thought He would give them lots of earthly things, things they could see and touch—but Jesus didn't give them any of those things they wanted. And they thought that if Jesus was God, then He ought to keep all the rules—those do's and don't's created by the religious leaders—but instead of following each and every Law, Jesus kept breaking them left and right.

"So even though Jesus made the entire world, people didn't recognize Who He was. The people in His own town didn't even believe in Him.

"But some of us did open our hearts to Him. And when we broke down the walls around our hearts, when we stopped living as though we each were the very center of the universe, Jesus made us a part of His kingdom. He made us children of God. Inside, we are like new people, as clean and innocent and loving as little babies. That's because you could say that through Jesus we've been 'born again.'

"Jesus' entire life showed us the love of God. That's because Jesus was God—God as a little baby. And, of course, then He grew and became a little boy who ran around and played and skinned His knees. He got hungry and He was sad sometimes, and He laughed a lot. He was just like you and me. And He was also God. He was never ever selfish, because He was love in human form.

"And that is the greatest miracle of all. All the other smaller miracles just helped us see the truth a little more clearly."

Rachel wrapped her arms around her knees. She had a sudden lonely feeling inside her heart that she didn't understand. The old man's story had been interesting enough, and Aaron was smiling at her now, his eyes bright with friendship. In Corinth, before she and her mother moved to Ephesus, the other children used to throw stones at her sometimes and make fun of her bare feet and ragged robe. Now that Aaron was her friend, no one ever teased her when she went through the market asking for food. So why should she be lonely?

She hunched her shoulders. Maybe it was just her hungry stomach that made her feel so empty. But she found herself wishing that she could have seen Jesus when He was a baby—or had Him for a Friend when He grew older.

He must have had rich parents, she decided, thinking about what the old man had said about Jesus, how He always told the truth and reached out to other people. Only a rich boy could do that. Someone poor like her had to protect herself—and she had to tell lies. How else could she take care of herself and her mother? She squinted her eyes and pushed the lonely feeling away. Why would she want to be friends with a spoiled rich boy?

"What are you thinking?" the old man asked her softly.

She shrugged. "All that stuff you said about Jesus not needing any walls around His heart. I bet He had lots of money, didn't He? Rich people can afford to be nice."

John laughed. "No," he said, "Jesus never had much money. In fact, His parents were so poor that He was born in a stable with the animals. And when He grew up, He never owned more than His robe and sandals. He didn't even have a home of His own."

Rachel's eyes widened with surprise. At least she and her mother had a place to sleep, even if it was tiny and dark and dirty. She shook her head. "Maybe that's why He didn't have any money then. Because He was too foolish to take care of Himself. People who are too trusting never end up with anything."

She heard Aaron take an indignant breath. "The Master wasn't foolish. He was wise and good and—"

John touched Aaron's shoulder gently. "The wisdom

of heaven looks like foolishness to those who live only in this world we see and touch."

Rachel pressed her lips together and glared at Aaron. It was easy enough for him to believe in this Jesus—after all, Aaron had a father who was alive and well, and his family had enough money to feed themselves. "I've got to go," she said stiffly. "I need to get to the marketplace. My mother wants me to buy bread and olives for tonight's supper." As she spoke the lie, she raised her head and stared into the old man's face.

He looked back at her, his eyes full of that peculiar love she had noticed earlier. She had the uncomfortable feeling, though, that he saw straight through her lie, and her face burned.

"Are you hungry?" he asked her.

"Not particularly," she said in a cold voice.

"Are you hungry?" he repeated.

She sighed. "I already said I'm not hungry." But her stomach betrayed her and growled loudly again, and she felt her face grow hotter.

The old man's gentle gaze never moved from her face. "I have some bread and cold meat inside that I was going to eat for my lunch. There is plenty there for all three of us." He smiled into Rachel's embarrassed eyes and asked her one more time, "Are you hungry?"

She drew her finger back and forth in the soft earth.

"Yes," she said at last.

John looked delighted with her answer. "There," he said softly. "Now I can get you something to eat." He got to his feet and slowly went inside.

While he was gone, Rachel kept her eyes on the lines she was drawing in the dust, but Aaron nudged her with his foot. "Why do you lie like that?" he asked her, his disgust plain in his voice. "It's silly."

"I know," she muttered. It had been a silly lie. After all, what she wanted was food, and saying she wasn't hungry wouldn't get her what she wanted. But sometimes she was ashamed to admit to her hunger. She hadn't wanted the old man to know just how poor she and her mother were.

John returned with bowls of food. Rachel and Aaron balanced them on their knees while the old man sat beside them on the bench. Rachel tried hard not to wolf the food, but there hadn't been any breakfast that morning, and the rolls were fresh and soft.

When she was finally full, she looked up at the old man. "Thank you," she said gruffly.

"You are welcome," he answered. "Do you understand why I asked you three times if you were hungry?"

She scowled and shook her head.

"Your lies built a tall wall around yourself. You thought you would be safe behind your wall, but you were scared, and so you built your wall higher still." He shook his head.

"We are all the same. And the truth is, until we break down our walls, until we dare to speak the truth, God cannot give us the good things He longs for us to have. We are too full of ourselves to have room for His blessings."

Rachel swallowed a last bite of bread. She wiped the crumbs from her mouth with the back of her hand. Now that she wasn't hungry anymore, she didn't feel as trembly inside, and she said loudly, "It's hard to care about all that stuff the priests and rabbis talk about in the synagogue—God's blessings and all that—when you're hungry." *There,* she thought defiantly, *if they want me to be honest, I'll be honest.*

"When I spoke of God's blessings," John said mildly, "I was referring to this." He touched a finger to the basket of leftover bread. "Food is certainly one of God's greatest blessings."

Rachel shook her head. Her father had studied the Law and the prophets every day, and he had often gone to the synagogue to listen to the rabbis—but he had never once mentioned to his daughter that God cared about something as ordinary as bread. She let out a small, sharp breath of laughter. "You mean eating and drinking is a part of your kingdom of heaven? I thought it was invisible. Do invisible people have to eat and drink?"

John laughed out loud, a delighted creaky chuckle, and even Aaron grinned. Rachel turned red again, afraid that they were laughing at her, but she could not mistake the kindness in the old man's eyes.

"We all can be a part of the Lord's kingdom," he said. "But that does not mean we will become invisible. And it certainly does not mean that we will stop eating and drinking. No, our bodies and all that we see and touch become a part of something bigger, something that means far more. God takes the things of this world and uses them for His kingdom. Eating and drinking were very important to Jesus."

Rachel muttered, "He must have been a jolly fat man."

Aaron kicked her, but John only laughed again. "No, He was not fat. We are not to make eating more important to us than God. But God does expect us to enjoy our food."

"Why would the Creator of the universe care if we like to eat?"

"Because He made us that way. He takes delight in what He has created."

Rachel narrowed her eyes at the old man. "How do you know all this? You sound as though everything you say is absolutely true, when really it's just your opinion." *Rachel,* her mother's voice scolded inside her head, *you're being rude,* but Rachel ignored her mother's warning.

John shook his head. "I know this is true, because I learned it from the Master Himself. And His miracles proved that God cares about food and drink."

"You mean that trick He did when He turned water into wine?"

Aaron let out an impatient sigh. "Grandfather John keeps telling you, Rachel—Jesus didn't do tricks. He wasn't a magician. He was real. Everything He did was true."

John nodded. "Let me tell you about the time the Master turned the water into wine. And then I will tell you about another time when He fed a crowd of more than five thousand people with just five loaves of bread and two small fishes."

Rachel frowned. "That's impossible."

But John just smiled and began to tell his story.

CHAPTER 3

"Right after Jesus asked me to be His disciple," John said, "He and some of the rest of us—Peter and Andrew, Philip and Nathanael, and myself—were all invited to attend a wedding outside of Nazareth in Cana. We were friends of the bridegroom, and we were looking forward to having a good time at the wedding party.

"Well, the wedding itself went just fine, and we were enjoying ourselves at the reception afterward, when all of a sudden people started whispering. 'Did you hear?' They were saying to each other, 'Can you imagine? They've run out of wine.'

"Everyone was laughing and gasping, and the poor bridegroom was bright red with embarrassment. After all, the bride-groom and his family are expected to provide a big party for everyone after a wedding. 'Do you suppose they're having money problems?' some people were whispering behind their hands.

" 'No,' said others. 'I hear they have plenty of gold. They are just too stingy to buy enough wine for all their guests. How selfish!'

"By this time, the bridegroom had turned redder still, his father was purple, and his mother was as white as her robe.

The bride looked like she might begin to cry at any moment.

"Peter and I turned to the Master, wondering what He would say. We knew Him well enough already to know that He wouldn't want people to be ruining the wedding celebration with their whispers and laughter. We were expecting Him to stand up and say something, maybe even scold the people nearest to Him who were busy gossiping.

"Right about then, though, Jesus' mother came hurrying up to Him, telling Him the whole story. We'd always seen how loving and respectful Jesus was to His mother, but now He just looked at her with a funny expression on His face.

" 'Woman,' He said, 'is that really any of our business?'

"At first, He seemed to be scolding her for being a part of all the gossip, though Mary wasn't really a gossipy sort of woman. But then He said, 'My time has not yet come.'

"At the time, I wasn't sure what He meant. But looking back now, I think He was reminding His mother that He always acted according to the kingdom of heaven's time frame rather than this world's schedule. I've noticed since then that we often think things should happen in a certain way at a certain time—but the kingdom's timing happens differently than we expect.

"Anyway, His mother seemed to understand what He meant. She gave Him a smile, and then she turned to the servants who were dishing out the food. 'Do whatever He tells you to do,' she told them softly.

"They gave her a strange look and kept right on with what they were doing. Peter and I and the rest of us went back to our food, resigned to the fact that there wouldn't be any more wine. And then Jesus got to His feet and walked over to the wall of the courtyard where six stone jars were standing in a row.

"He stood there for a moment looking at those jars, studying them, with an odd sort of smile on His face. He looked as though He might laugh right out loud, though I couldn't see anything particularly funny about those jars. They were those big tall ones that hold twenty or thirty gallons, and we'd all washed our hands in that water before we ate, the way the Law requires that we do. So now they had been pushed out of the way along the wall and were standing there empty.

"Jesus motioned to the servants, who by now had finished serving the meal. 'Fill the jars with water,' He told them.

"They gave Him a surprised look, because after all, there really wasn't much point in anyone washing their hands in the middle of a meal. Some of them knew Mary, so they turned to her, and she kind of waved her hand at them, telling them again to do whatever her Son told them to do. So finally, they shrugged their shoulders and filled the jars up to the brim with water.

"We were all expecting that Jesus would want us to

wash our hands now, so we put down our meat and the fruits we were eating, and we wiped our greasy hands on our napkins. I suppose we thought that Jesus wanted to talk to us about getting our hearts clean—especially after all the unkind words that had been said about the bridegroom—and we figured that washing our hands again was Jesus' way of showing us what He meant. Or maybe we even thought that He wanted us to stop the celebration altogether.

"But Jesus took us totally by surprise. He pointed to one of the jars of water and said, 'Pour out some now and take it to the master of ceremonies.'

"The servants raised their eyebrows at this, but Mary motioned to them again, and so they did what Jesus asked. And then those of us who were closest noticed something very strange about the water that came out of the jar. We had seen it go in looking just like everyday water, clear and ordinary. But now it looked darker somehow, and thicker. And it smelled like. . .well, it smelled like wine.

"We all got very quiet, and we watched while the servant carried a cup to the master of ceremonies. He was whispering busily to the bridegroom's father, and he looked impatient from being interrupted, but he took a sip from the cup. And then his face lit up.

" 'This is wonderful!' he cried. He called to the bridegroom to come over, and then he slapped his friend on the back. 'Usually a host serves the best wine first. Then, when everyone is full and doesn't care, he brings out the less expensive wine. You had us thinking the wine was all gone. But you were simply saving the best wine until now!'

"And that was the first miracle Jesus ever performed. It was the first sign He gave us of what the kingdom of heaven is really like—a place of bounty and richness, a place where there is plenty of God's best for everyone."

John paused for a moment, allowing his words to sink into the hearts of his young listeners. Then he began another story:

"After the other disciples and I had been following Jesus for quite some time, one spring morning Jesus suggested that we try to get away from the crowds of people for awhile. We could tell He was tired, and we all were looking forward to having some time to relax. So we set off in our fishing boat for the far side of the Sea of Galilee, and then we all sat down together on the hillside. The sun was shining, the grass was fresh and green, and the wind off the sea was warm and soft against our faces. We lay back in the sunshine, happy just to be there with the Master.

"But just as were settling down, Jesus pointed to the shore. Wouldn't you know it, the people had gotten wind of where we were heading, and they had followed us there. Peter and Andrew moaned and rolled their eyes when they saw that there would be no escaping the crowd, at least not that day. Jesus didn't speak a word of complaint, though.

"But He did turn to Philip and ask, 'How will we feed all these people?' The way He said it wasn't like He was grumbling or like He thought there was no good answer to the question. He sounded like He really wanted Philip to tell Him, but looking back, I suspect He already knew what He was going to do; He was just testing Philip.

"Well, Philip shrugged his shoulders, because he didn't see any possible answer to Jesus' question. He looked out at the size of the crowd that was headed our way, and he sighed. 'There must be five thousand families out there. Even if we had two hundred denarii—and we don't—we still wouldn't have enough to give each person even a bite of bread.' He sounded a little exasperated that Jesus even asked the question.

"Meanwhile, though, Andrew had been moving around in the crowd, talking to the people, and now he came back and dropped down at Jesus' feet. 'There's a boy here who has five barley loaves and two fishes,' he said.

"Some of us laughed out loud, and some of us just looked at him, wondering why he was being so silly to even tell us about such a small amount of food. Andrew spread out his hands. 'I know, I know. That's nothing among so many people. I just thought I'd mention it.'

"But Jesus got to His feet, and He looked as though He

thought the problem had been solved. 'Bring the boy to Me,' He said.

"Andrew led the boy through the crowd, and Jesus knelt down beside him. 'I hear you brought a lunch today,' He said to the boy.

"The boy nodded, looking shy. He held out the basket of food for Jesus to see.

" 'That's a good-looking lunch,' Jesus said. 'May I have it?' He asked.

"The boy hesitated for just a second. He looked down at his food, and you could tell he had been looking forward to eating it. Then he nodded and silently put the basket in Jesus' hands. Jesus smiled at him.

" 'Thank you,' He said, and then He turned to us. 'Tell the people to have a seat on the grass. They might as well be comfortable while they eat.'

"When everyone was sitting down, Jesus said a blessing over that tiny basket of food, thanking God for what He had given to us through the boy. The crowd was completely silent, watching Him, wondering what He was doing. He began to break the bread into pieces, and you could hear people start to whisper. They must have wondered if Jesus had lost His mind.

"But then He started passing the bread out to the people—and this was amazing—there was enough for everyone there, every father, every mother, every child! When each person had some bread, Jesus turned to the fish and did the same thing. And again, as He passed the fish out, there was plenty for every person there. Not just a bite, or a little snack to tide them over until they could go home and get something better to eat—no, the people all ate until they were full. You should have seen how excited that little boy was when he realized his lunch had fed so many people!

"When everyone had had enough, Jesus turned to us, and with a voice filled with laughter, He said, 'Collect the leftovers now. We don't want to waste anything.'

"So we did, and we each came back with a basket full of food, enough for us all to have a lunch of our own.

"You should have heard the crowd buzzing. 'This must be a prophet that has come into the world,' they were saying—and then they went even further and started talking about crowning Jesus king. But Jesus slipped off into the hills by Himself.

"Well, the other disciples and I waited all afternoon for Him to come back, but as night began to fall we could see a storm was coming up, and we wanted to get the boat back in port. At last we left without Him, figuring He wanted some time to be alone, the way He did sometimes. We rowed about three or four miles, with the wind growing stronger all the time, and we were beginning to think we would never get across the sea. It was really frightening.

"Just then we looked out across the waves, and we saw

the strangest thing. Someone was walking on the water, coming steadily toward us, stepping over those waves as though they were as solid as earth! Goose bumps popped up on my arms, and I could see Andrew's hair literally stand on end.

"And then we heard a familiar voice calling to us through the noise of the storm. 'It's Me. Don't be scared.'

"As soon as I heard that voice, I stopped being afraid, but I was still overwhelmed with awe. By that time, I'd seen Jesus do plenty of marvelous things—but nothing as strange as walking on water. I knew then that Jesus was more than just a teacher, more than a prophet even. He really was the Creator Himself, the Son of God.

"Well, we pulled Him up into the boat, and another weird thing happened then; instantly, as soon as He was in the boat with us, we reached the dock we'd been struggling toward. It was like we simply slipped through space all of a sudden, and there we were.

"By then, we were all too tired to ask any questions; we just fell asleep on the boat. But when morning came, the crowd caught up with us again. They had seen that Jesus had not left with us the night before, so they couldn't figure out how He had gotten there.

"He didn't answer their questions, though. Instead, He said to them, 'You don't really care how I got here. And all My miracles aren't really the thing that interests you most. You're following Me because I satisfied your hunger yesterday. Don't search for the sort of food that will spoil, but seek the food that lasts forever, the food of eternal life.'

"By this time, we had all seen so many strange things, that it wouldn't have seemed any stranger to us if Jesus had produced some magical, marvelous source of food that would never rot, that would last forever. So someone asked Him, 'Can You prove that You can do what You're telling us?' And someone else said, 'Moses fed our ancestors manna from heaven. Are You going to give us something like that?' And yet another person asked, 'How can we work for this food? What should we do?'

"Jesus looked out at the faces in the crowd for a moment, as though He were thinking of the right words to make them comprehend. Then He sighed and shook His head, as though He knew we still weren't really ready to understand Him. 'The truth is,' He said quietly, 'what Moses did was not all that important. God gives you the real bread from heaven. The bread that God gives comes down from heaven and gives life to the world.'

"At that, everyone started shouting out, 'Sir, please, give us this bread that You're talking about! We want it now and for always. That way we could feed our families. None of us would ever be hungry again.'

"Jesus just smiled. 'I am the Bread of Life,' He said. 'Whoever comes to Me will never be hungry again, and whoever believes in Me will never be thirsty again. Everything that My Father gives to Me, I will pass along to you, and I will never turn anyone away. I have come down from heaven, not to do what I want to do, but to do what My Father wants Me to do. And what He wants is to give you all eternal life.'

"At this, the Jewish leaders in the crowd began to mutter, 'Just Who does He think He is, saying He came down from heaven? After all, we know His mother and father. He's Joseph and Mary's son. What is all this talk about magical bread from heaven?'

"Jesus was still smiling, but He shook His head now. 'The only way you are ever going to know God is through Me. I'm not talking about the sort of miracle that Moses did when he gave you manna in the desert, and I'm not talking about the sort of bread that we eat every day. That kind of bread only satisfies your hunger for a little while, and in the end you'll still die. I'm speaking of a different sort of bread altogether, a bread that will make you live forever. I am that bread. The bread that I give you is Myself, My body. I give it away to be the life for the whole world.'

"By this time, as you can imagine, we were all pretty confused. We'd seen Jesus give us real, actual bread, the kind you can sink your teeth into, the kind that fills your stomach. But He was talking about another kind of bread, a bread that was just as real, maybe more so.

"One thing we did know, though. Just like Jesus had

made that little boy's bread be enough for everyone, we knew there also would be plenty of this eternal bread He was talking about. No one would be left out, and all could help themselves. All they had to do was come to Jesus— and He would feed them Himself. Then they would live forever."

CHAPTER 4

Rachel shook her head. "Well, I'm still confused. What was He talking about when He said He was bread and people had to eat Him? It sounds pretty weird to me."

John let out a breath of laughter. "We felt the same way at the time. Some of Jesus' followers came right out and said, 'This is more than we can understand. Why are we even bothering to listen to such silly talk?' "

"So what did Jesus tell them?" Rachel asked. She was surprised to discover she really wanted to know; she was growing more and more interested in this strange man, Jesus of Nazareth.

John looked down into her face. What he saw there seemed to please him, for he smiled as he said, "Jesus asked us, 'So this shocks you, does it? What if one day you see Me going back to the place where I came from? Will you finally understand then?' He sort of sighed and then He tried again to explain to us. He wasn't talking about earthly food, you see, not the sort of thing you and I and Aaron just ate together. Real food, eternal food, is the sort that belongs to the kingdom of heaven, the invisible world of the spirit. That world is tied to this one—that's why Jesus used that little boy's bread and fish, because He was showing us that He can use any of the things we see and touch, no matter how small they seem to us. But the kingdom of heaven goes far beyond this world. It's more real than anything you can see or touch, and it lasts forever. And when we give everything we have in this world, then Jesus uses it for His kingdom— and He gives us Himself in return. And then our hearts are never hungry again."

Rachel scowled down at her dirty toes, trying hard to understand. She could almost catch a glimmer of what John was talking about, but just as she thought she had it, it slipped away, leaving her frustrated. "It doesn't make sense," she burst out.

"No," John agreed, "it doesn't. Not when you look at it from one point of view. But from another point of view— the kingdom's viewpoint—it makes perfect sense."

"But what good does it do me?" Rachel cried, her cheeks bright red. "What good will Jesus do my mother and me? We'll still be hungry and poor."

John nodded gravely. "Yes, you may be, though that is not what God wants for His people. But in this world, we do suffer. We get hungry and sick. We even die. But when your heart belongs to Jesus and His kingdom, you begin to look at all those things differently."

Rachel drew her toes back and forth in the dust. "My father got sick and died," she muttered. "How am I supposed to look at that any differently?"

Aaron leaned forward and touched Rachel's arm. "Maybe it helps if you keep remembering that this world isn't the end," he said, his voice sounding gruff and shy. "In the kingdom of heaven God wants us all to be whole and healthy." He glanced at his grandfather. "Isn't that right, Grandfather John?"

The old man nodded. "One day in God's kingdom we will all be completely well, completely healthy, exactly the way God wants us to be."

Rachel blinked tears out of her eyes and raised her chin high. "How do you know?" she asked bitterly. "Oh, it sounds good. It's what we'd all like to believe, isn't it? But how do you know?"

John spread his hands out. "I know because the Master told me. He showed me with His miracles."

Rachel turned her head and looked at the old man. "So now you're going to tell me that Jesus could make sick people healthy?"

John nodded. "Yes, He could. He did so many times. Let me tell you about three of the people whom Jesus made well."

John clasped his hands behind his head, and began his story:

"We had been traveling around Judea quite a bit, Jesus and the twelve of us, when Jesus decided to go back to Galilee to see His mother and the rest of His family. While we were there, we visited Cana again, the same town where Jesus had turned the water into wine.

"A royal officer happened to be in Cana on business while we were there. This man was in a hurry to get back home, because his little boy was very sick. But when the officer heard that Jesus was in town, he came to Him and said, 'Please, come home with me to Capernaum. My little boy is there, and when I left him he was so sick that I'm afraid he may not live much longer. Please. . .please hurry. Come home with me and cure him.' His voice was choked with tears. 'He's just a little boy. . .and we love him so much. Please come with me and make him well again.'

"This wasn't the first time Jesus had healed someone, you see, and by this time He had quite a reputation. We were always being crowded with sick people who stretched out their hands to Jesus, trying to get close to Him, trying just to touch Him. There was something wonderful about Him, something that flowed out of Him, that made everyone well again.

"But this time Jesus looked at the man for a long time, and then He shook His head. 'I'm not a magician. Why won't you believe in Me without Me doing a work of power?'

"You see, I suppose that royal officer was like a lot of us: He wanted Jesus to do something for him. He didn't want to just follow Jesus, no matter what happened, even if his son died.

"Well, Jesus kept on looking into the man's face. His eyes were stern at first, but then they softened. 'Go on home,' He said gently to the officer. 'I don't need to come with you. Your son will live.'

"The man took a deep breath, as though a heavy load had dropped off his shoulders, and a look of joy spread across his face. 'Thank You, Lord,' he whispered, and then he hurried away.

"We all wondered what had happened, so when I bumped into that officer a few weeks later, I asked him how his son was.

"He gave me a big smile. 'He's fine, just fine. As good as new. The Lord healed him.'

"And then he told me what had happened. After he left Cana, when he was still a ways off from Capernaum, he saw two of his servants riding out to meet him. His heart sank, for he was afraid they had been sent to call him home for his son's funeral. But when they got close enough that he could see their faces, he saw they were smiling.

" 'Your boy is going to live!' they shouted to him. 'The fever has broken, and he is sitting up and eating food.'

"Tears of joy rolled down the man's face. 'When did he begin to recover?' he asked them.

" 'It was the strangest thing,' they told him. 'Yesterday morning we thought the boy wouldn't live through the day. And then at one in the afternoon, the fever suddenly left him.'

"The man thought back, and he realized that one in the afternoon was the exact moment when Jesus had told him that his son would live. He hurried home to see his son, and he and his whole family and all of his servants believed in Jesus from that day on.

"Another time when we were in Galilee, we stopped at Capernaum. The royal officer was delighted to see Jesus again, and news that the Master was in town spread pretty quickly. Before long, the house where we were staying was so packed with people that you couldn't have squeezed in even one more skinny child. There was just a little space in the middle of the room, around where Jesus was standing, so He just had room enough to take a breath while He spoke.

"I was packed in with the rest, with someone's elbow in my back and my toes squashed by the old man next to me. The Master was preaching, and I was listening, when all of a sudden a funny noise above my head made me lose track of what He was saying. It was a scratchy, scraping sort of noise, and all I could think was that a rat was up there, crawling around in the rafters.

"I turned back to Jesus and tried to concentrate—but the next thing I knew, bits of something were falling on my head. Everyone was looking up at the ceiling now, and the Master stopped talking. When I glanced at Him, I saw He was looking up, too, with an expression of amusement and welcome on His face.

" 'What's happening?' Peter muttered in my ear. But, of course, I didn't know any more than he did.

"Chunks of clay were dropping down on the floor from the ceiling, and people were jumping out of the way. Now there was a hole up there big enough for us to see the sky. And then the hole got bigger yet, a long rectangle large enough that four men could lower another man down through to the space on the floor in front of Jesus.

"You see, these four men had tried to bring their friend to the Master for healing. Their friend had done plenty of bad things in his day, but they loved him anyway, and now that he was paralyzed, they helped take care of him. When they found that the house was too jam-packed for them to bring their friend to Jesus, they didn't let that stop them. No, they just carried their friend up on the roof and dug a hole through the clay bricks.

"Jesus bent over the paralyzed man. 'My son,' He said, 'your sins are forgiven.'

"There were some religious leaders in the house that day, and I heard them hiss when Jesus said this. 'What?' they muttered to each other. 'He's blaspheming. God is the only One who can forgive sins.'

"Jesus must have heard what they were saying, because He turned to them and said, 'Why are you so upset about what I just said? Do you think it is easier for Me to say to this man, "Your sins are forgiven"?—or "Get up, pick up your mat, and walk"?' Jesus shook His head, looking like He didn't know whether to laugh or let out a big sigh of exasperation. 'All right,' He said at last. 'Let Me prove to you that I, the Son of Man, truly do have the authority here on earth to forgive sins.' He turned back to the paralyzed man on the floor and bent down to him. 'Stand up, Son,' Jesus said softly. 'Pick up your mat and go on home. You are healed.'

"The man just stared up at Jesus for a moment, a stunned look on his face, and then he leapt to his feet with a cry of joy. The crowd around him stood frozen as he pushed his way through. The last we heard of him, he was laughing and calling out the good news to his friends.

"The rest of us began to shout and praise God. 'I've never seen anything like this ever before!' the old man next to me exclaimed.

"I nodded my head. By that time, I had seen Jesus heal plenty of people—but I could never get over the wonder of it. Each time I was filled with awe, and each time I found myself loving my Master even more than I had before.

"A little while after that, we all went up to Jerusalem for one of the Jewish festivals. While we were there, we went by the Sheep Pool, the place they call Bethesda. The story goes that an angel comes down every now and then and stirs up the water, and afterward the first person to jump into the pool will be healed of whatever diseases he or she might have—so sick people all would go there to be healed. The day we happened by was no different. Sick people were lying all over the ground, people who were blind or could not walk or were paralyzed. Their families brought them there and then waited with them in case a miracle would happen in the water.

"The twelve of us were going to go on by, but Jesus walked right into that crowd of sick people. He squatted next to a man who was lying on a blanket beside his crutch, and Jesus began to talk to him. It turned out that this man had been crippled for thirty-eight years.

" 'Do you want to be healed?' Jesus asked him.

"The man shrugged. 'Of course I do. But I don't have any family to help me get into the pool. While I'm hobbling along with this,' he made a face at his crutch, 'someone else always gets ahead of me.'

"Jesus got to His feet, and then He held His hand out to the man. 'Come on. Leave your crutch there—you don't need it anymore. Just get to your feet, pick up your blanket—and let's go.'

"The man looked up at Jesus for just a second, and then his face broke into a grin. Just like that, he jumped to his feet. He was completely healed.

"Later, Jesus talked to the man in the temple. 'Now that you are well,' He told him, 'stop living just for yourself. If you don't change the way you live, you may end up even sicker than you were before.'

"You see, Jesus was trying to show the man that our bodies' sicknesses really don't matter all that much. It's what is in our hearts that is really important.

"Now, this last miracle took place on the Sabbath, and that made the Jewish leaders angry with Jesus. They said He was disobeying the Law, you see, by doing work on the Sabbath.

"But Jesus told them, 'My Father is always working in His creation, and I am working, too.'

"Of course, this just made the Jewish leaders that much angrier with Him, because now Jesus was not only breaking the Sabbath, He was also claiming that God was His Father. But Jesus only gave them a little smile and said, 'I am simply doing what God does. His love works through Me. God gives life, and so do I. If you believe what I'm saying, then you don't have to wait for eternal life—you have already gotten hold of it, and it's yours. Nothing I do is selfish, nothing I do is about Me—everything I do is done from love, and that is the message I bring you. That is what Moses was trying to tell you in the first place, when he gave you the Law. But you don't believe Moses, so how can you believe what I'm trying to tell you now?'

"Those Jewish leaders obviously didn't have a clue what He was talking about. They just turned away, their faces hard and angry, and they began to plot how they could get rid of Jesus.

"But the rest of us thought a lot about what Jesus had said. And as we watched Him heal person after person, we started to understand that Jesus wanted to heal not only our bodies, but our hearts. He wanted to make us whole on the inside, too. He wanted to teach us how to love."

Rachel twisted a corner of her robe between her fingers as she thought about the stories John had told. "I already know how to love," she said at last.

"Do you?" John asked.

She glanced at him. "Of course I do. I love my mother."

"That is a start," the old man said gently. "A very good start. But does love control your life? Do you lay down your life for your mother?"

"Of course I—" Rachel shut her mouth in the middle of her sentence, for she suddenly remembered the night before when she had shouted at her mother and refused to sweep the floor. *But that doesn't mean I wouldn't die for my mother,* she told herself, *not if I had to.* Little things like sweeping the floor weren't that important. *Or are they?* she wondered, looking at John's lined face.

"And what about the people in the marketplace?" the old man prodded. "Do you love them?"

Rachel thought of the faces of the vendors at the market. They were kinder to her now that Aaron was her friend, but she still remembered the way they had looked at her when she had first moved to Ephesus. "Get away, you dirty brat!" one woman had shouted at her when Rachel had asked her for some food. Rachel had been very hungry that day, and her mother had been sick; Rachel had next tried to steal some grapes, and a man had chased her and hit her so hard across the head that her ears had rung.

"No," Rachel said between her teeth. "I don't love them. Why should I? They don't love me."

John nodded. "You see, you don't know how to love yet. True love lays itself down, every day, in the smallest and the biggest ways. True love gives and never steals, no matter what. That is the sort of love that Jesus teaches. That is the sort of love He brought to us. That is what He was showing us as He healed the sick when He was here on earth."

Rachel shook her head. She was thinking about her father, remembering the long year before he died. "When my father was sick, my mother went to the temple every day and prayed that he would get better. And then one day, he was better. For three whole months, we thought the disease was gone. My mother and father praised God. We were so happy. . . ." Rachel blinked her eyes, remembering. "But then he got sick again. And this time he didn't get better, no matter how hard we prayed. This time he died." She looked up at the old man. "Those people that Jesus healed—did they stay healed?"

John nodded. "Yes, I believe they did. But, Child, that doesn't mean that eventually they won't die. They weren't given new bodies. By now the officer's boy has grown older, and one day he will die. And the paralyzed man and the man who was a cripple will also die sooner or later, if they have not died already. That is the way these earthly bodies of ours are made."

Rachel's fingers curled into fists. "So what good did it do? What was the point of Jesus healing them when in the end they'll just die anyway? You keep talking about people living forever, but I don't see that happening anywhere. Even Jesus got killed in the end. And look at you—you were one of His best friends, but you're an old man and—"

Aaron kicked her, and she broke off, but John only smiled. "Yes, I, too, will die before too long. I will hate to leave the people I love," he said as he touched Aaron's shoulder, "but I am looking forward to life in the world to come. I know that my Master is the Lord of both life and death, and nothing can ever separate me from His love."

The hungry, empty feeling inside Rachel's heart was back again, but she tried to pretend she felt nothing but impatience. "You can't know that for sure," she spit out. "Your Master may have turned water into wine and fed people and even healed people, but you can't tell me He made anyone live forever."

"No," John said, "not in the way you mean. But He did bring someone back to life."

Before Rachel could protest, John started his story.

"One of the Master's good friends was a man named Lazarus. Lazarus lived with his two sisters, Mary and Martha, in Bethany; and many times we would go to their house for a time of rest and fun. But one day we got a message from Mary and Martha that their brother was very sick.

"We were all upset and worried to hear the bad news, but Jesus said to us, 'This sickness that Lazarus has won't end in death. No, the reason for him getting sick has to do with God's glory. God wants to show people what He is really like.'

"So we didn't leave for Bethany the way we had thought we might when we got the news. Instead, we stayed where we were until a couple of days later when Jesus suddenly announced, 'Let's go back to Judea now.'

"We disciples weren't so sure that was a good idea. After all, the last time we'd been in Judea, the Jewish leaders had tried to kill Jesus. But when we suggested to Jesus that maybe this wasn't such a smart time for making a trip, He said, 'Our friend Lazarus has fallen asleep. I need to go and wake him up.'

"That explained why Jesus suddenly wanted to go to Judea, because Bethany was in Judea, after all; but it seemed a little silly to us. After all, we hadn't made the trip when we first heard Lazarus was sick, so we couldn't see why we should go now. We all exchanged glances, and then one of us said, 'But, Master, if he's been sick, then sleeping will do him good. If he's resting comfortably, it probably means he's getting over his sickness. We can visit him later when he's all better.'

"But Jesus shook His head, and then He stopped talking in riddles and told us, 'Lazarus is dead. For your sakes, I'm glad I wasn't there, because this will give you another chance to understand Who I really am. Come on, now. Let's go see Lazarus.'

"Well, we disciples just looked at each other again. Jesus was always throwing us off balance like that, saying and doing things that seemed to make no sense. And we really were scared to have Jesus go back to Judea where He had so many enemies.

"After a moment, though, Thomas shrugged his shoulders. 'Come on then,' he said and sighed. 'We might as well go with Him. If we have to, we can die with Him, but let's go.'

"So we did. We went to Judea, and we managed to avoid running into any of the Jewish leaders. But when we reached Bethany, we found out that Lazarus had been dead for four days. The place was crowded with people who had come to pay their respects to Mary and Martha.

"Martha must have gotten word from someone that Jesus was on His way, because she came out to meet us while we were still on the edge of town. When Jesus saw her coming toward Him, He stopped walking and just looked at her. She looked right back at Him, her face all wet with tears. 'Master,' she said, 'if You had only been here, my brother wouldn't have died. I know that God will do whatever You ask.'

"Jesus reached out and touched her face. 'Your brother will live again,' He said gently.

"Martha sniffed back her tears. 'Yes. I know. We will all live again on resurrection day.' But you could tell she was just repeating the words she had heard all her life in the synagogue; she didn't really know what those words meant, and they weren't much comfort to her right then.

"Jesus smiled. 'I am the resurrection and the life. Those who believe in Me, even though they die like everyone else, will live again. Because they follow Me, they will live forever, and they will never truly die. Do you believe this, Martha?'

"She nodded. 'I have always believed You are the Messiah, the Son of God, the One who has come into the world from God.'

"Jesus gave her a hug. 'I'm glad you believe, Martha.' He looked into her face for a moment, and you could see He was pleased with what He saw there. Then He gave her a little push. 'Go get your sister for Me. I need to talk to her as well.'

"So Martha went to get Mary, and Jesus waited for her there on the road. Pretty soon, we saw Mary coming toward us, followed by a crowd of mourners. Everyone was sobbing out loud and wailing, and Mary's face was blotched and swollen with tears. She threw herself at Jesus' feet, not seeming to care that she was getting her face and hands all dirty.

" 'Lord,' she blurted, 'if You had been here, my brother wouldn't have died.' She was sobbing too hard to say anything more.

"As Jesus looked down at her, His expression became troubled. 'Where have you put him?' he asked Mary, and we all heard the catch in His voice.

"She pulled herself to her feet, but she was still crying too much to talk. 'Come and see,' one of her relatives said to the Master.

"As we followed the crowd toward Lazarus's grave, we were feeling pretty sad. Lazarus had been a good friend to us all, and it didn't seem possible that he wouldn't be coming out to greet us soon. Tears were rolling down our own faces, and when I looked over at Jesus, I saw that He was crying, too.

"I knew how much Jesus had loved Lazarus, so I guess I wasn't surprised, but the crowd all started nudging each other and pointing at Jesus' face, murmuring to themselves. Mostly they were sympathetic of Jesus' grief, but I heard someone say, 'This man healed everyone else. Why couldn't He keep His own friend from dying?'

"By this time we reached the cave where they had put Lazarus's body, and I could see that Jesus was really upset. He wiped His hand across His eyes, though, and straightened His shoulders. 'Roll the stone away from the grave's opening,' He called out.

"Like I said, sometimes the things the Master did or said just didn't make much sense. We all just stared at Him. Martha had joined us again, though, and she put her hands on her hips and shook her head. 'Why would You want to open that grave, Lord? By now the smell will be terrible. After all, he's been dead four days now, and the weather's been hot.'

"Martha was always a practical one; she believed in telling things like they were. The Master smiled at her through His tears. 'Didn't I always say that if you really believe, you will see God's glory?'

"Martha stared back at Him for a second, and then she waved her hands at the crowd. 'Go ahead,' she said. 'You heard Him. Roll the stone away.'

"So they did, and everyone stood there as still as could be, wondering what would happen next. Mary had stopped crying and was looking at Jesus with an expression of wonder and relief, but Martha's face was perfectly blank, as though she were afraid to hope.

"Jesus looked up at the sky and began to pray out loud. 'Father,' He said, 'thank You for hearing Me. Of course You and I both know that You always hear me, but I'm saying it out loud for the benefit of this crowd of people standing here listening. I want them to see that You really did send Me to them.'

"Jesus' tears had disappeared now, and His face was shining with joy. He took a step toward the grave and leaned into the dark hole. 'Lazarus,' He shouted, 'you can come out now!' He sounded as though Lazarus were a child who was simply hiding in that grave, and now the game was over and it was time for Lazarus to come out for supper. Jesus had a way of saying the most extraordinary things in the most ordinary voice, as though it were all perfectly normal. Listening to Him, I would realize that from the Master's perspective, all His miracles were completely normal; they were exactly the way things ought to be, and the rest of the broken world was what was abnormal.

"Anyway, when He told Lazarus to come out of the grave, everything was absolutely still at first; none of us even dared to breathe. And then we heard something, a sort of rustling, shuffling sound, and the hairs on my arms stood straight up. And the next thing we knew, there was Lazarus in the mouth of the grave, on his feet, all wrapped up in the grave clothes, with his face covered by the head cloth. None of us could move a muscle.

"And then Lazarus broke our spell. 'Let me out!' he said, sounding grumpy and confused.

"Jesus began to laugh. 'Unwrap him and let him go!'

"You see, Jesus wanted us to know exactly what His kingdom is like. It's a place where everyone is satisfied; there is plenty of what everyone needs and more than enough to go around. It's a place filled with overflowing joy, where no one is sick or damaged or wounded. Everyone there is whole and complete, exactly what God intended them to be from the beginning of Creation. And when Jesus raised Lazarus, He showed us that on top of all that, His kingdom is a place where death no longer exists. Jesus is God's Son, and the power of His love is even greater than death."

CHAPTER 6

Rachel had a funny feeling inside her. It felt a little like when she was looking forward to something really nice happening, and it was something like the way she felt when her mother held her on her lap, even though Rachel was really too big for that now. But mostly it felt too good to be true, because Rachel had learned that usually the good things you hope for never happen, and almost always bad things happen instead. She frowned, trying to ignore the funny feeling that made her want to smile up at John.

"There's just one problem with everything you've said," she told the old man in a small, flat voice. "In the end, Jesus' invisible kingdom didn't do Him any good. Because no matter how pretty it all sounds, it doesn't do any of us any good. It's just not real."

Aaron let out a yelp of protest. "How can you say that? After everything Grandfather John has told you? Don't you understand yet?" He shook his head, as though he couldn't believe how slow she was.

Rachel's cheeks flushed. "You can believe whatever makes you happy, Aaron," she said between her teeth. "But I'm too old to waste my time with make-believe."

"But Jesus is real," Aaron said. "Grandfather John saw

all these things happen with his own eyes. They're all true."

Rachel shrugged. "So what? Jesus was real. He's dead now."

"No, no, He's not!" Aaron turned to John. "Tell her, Grandfather."

The old man smiled at the two children. "Remember what Jesus told Martha? He said that He is the resurrection and the life. Remember how I told you that Jesus was there when the world was created? Well, that same life that made everything in the beginning is still working now. That same life, that same power will save us from death. Because that life and that power is Jesus. And He gives His life to all who give their lives to Him. Even though these bodies will one day die, the eternal part of us will live forever."

Rachel made a face. "Sure. You can believe whatever you want about what happens after we die. No one can contradict you, because except for this Lazarus, no one has ever come back to tell people what happens when we die." She shook her head and folded her arms tight across her chest. "Maybe this Master of yours had some sort of funny power. Maybe He really could turn water into wine and feed thousands of people with just one little boy's lunch. Maybe He could make sick people get better, and maybe He could even bring people back to life again when their bodies were already all stinky and rotten. But, like I said, what good did it do Him? In the end, He couldn't save Himself. In the end, they killed Him. Right?"

"Yes," John said gravely. "They killed Him on a cross outside Jerusalem. Just as we had feared, the Jewish leaders put Him to death. They murdered the giver of all life."

Aaron sat up straight, his eyes shining. "But that's not the end of the story, is it, Grandfather John?" He grinned at Rachel, then turned back to his grandfather. "Tell her what happened next."

"I'd be glad to tell her, Aaron," John said. And he began a final story for the children.

"All along, Jesus had been warning us that He was going to die, but I guess we didn't want to hear Him. After all, we believed He was the Messiah—and the Messiah wouldn't die before he got a chance to be king. According to everything we'd always been taught, the Messiah was the person who would win. He'd kill God's enemies with his super-human power, and then he would set up his kingdom. So when Jesus told us He was planning on dying as part of His mission here on earth, it just didn't make any sense to us. It was one more of those weird things He was always saying, and because we couldn't understand it, we pretty much ignored Him whenever He'd start talking about His death.

"The thing was, though, all along, He had also said that He would rise again. But until it really happened, we just didn't understand what He was trying to tell us. Because this was the most important miracle of all, the one that made sense of all the others.

"So first of all, I guess you need to know that Jesus was really dead. I saw Him nailed up on that cross; I was there, and I saw His blood and His pain. It was the worst day of my life. He was the best Friend I had ever had, and I believed He was the Son of God. I just couldn't understand how such a terrible thing could be happening. It seemed like a nightmare. It couldn't be true. Jesus couldn't die.

"But He did. I saw the exact moment when the spirit left His body. His head dropped, and His eyes went blank; He stopped breathing, and we knew life had left Him. A soldier came and stuck a spear in Him. I was an eyewitness to all this.

"Later on, a couple of Jesus' followers who had some money, Joseph of Arimathea and Nicodemus, got permission to take Jesus' body down from the cross. Together, they took the body and buried it in a garden nearby. We all went home, feeling as dark and hopeless as we had ever felt. 'What was the point of everything He taught,' we were saying to each other, 'if in the end He couldn't keep Himself from being killed?'

"Those next couple of nights, I lay awake in the darkness, trying to make sense out of everything that had happened. But I couldn't. I was too sad.

"But early on Sunday morning, Peter and I were trying

to choke down some breakfast, when Mary Magdalene came running in, all upset, panting so hard she almost couldn't speak. She had run all the way from Jesus' grave, it turned out, and when she had caught her breath, she gasped, 'Someone rolled the stone away from His grave!'

" 'What are you talking about?' we asked her.

"She inhaled a deep breath. 'It's true. And whoever did it must have taken the Lord's body. He's not in the tomb. I don't know where they have put Him!'

"She began to cry, but I was filled with a sudden wild hope. I was remembering another tomb with a rolled back stone, you see, and I was thinking of the way Jesus had laughed with delight when Lazarus came stumbling out of his tomb. So I jumped to my feet, and Peter and I raced to the grave where Joseph and Nicodemus had buried Jesus.

"I have to confess that I beat Peter in the race to get there first—and sure enough, just like Mary had said, someone had rolled the stone away from the mouth of the tomb. I bent over and looked inside. I could see the grave clothes lying where the body should have been, but they were empty. The face cloth was lying to one side, all neatly folded, as though Jesus had gotten up that morning and remembered to make the bed before He went out for the day. Suddenly, I was laughing and crying, all at the same time.

"Then Peter caught up with me and pushed past me. He went inside the grave and looked at the empty grave clothes.

I followed him, and we just stood there, staring down at those linen cloths, not daring to say out loud what we were both thinking.

"Finally, we went back home, but we could hardly concentrate on anything. We had that excited feeling in our hearts that something wonderful, something amazing, was about to happen. Or maybe it already had happened.

"Later that afternoon, Mary Magdalene stopped by again. Her eyes were shining, and we knew we were right: Something wonderful had happened, something that was better than we had ever imagined.

" 'I've seen Him!' she cried. 'He's alive!'

"I can't describe the joy that swept through me then. We jumped to our feet, demanding that she tell us everything that had happened.

"She had gone back to the grave after Peter and I went home, and she had stood there crying, wondering where Jesus' body had gone. Something made her look inside the grave, just as we had, but this time two angels in white robes were sitting at each end of the place where the body should have been. She nearly jumped out of her skin, but the angels just looked at her, their faces calm and glowing.

" 'Why are you crying?' they asked her.

"She wiped her nose on her sleeve and gulped back her tears. 'Because,' she said, 'someone has taken away my Lord, and I don't know where they've put Him.'

"Before the angels could answer her, though, she saw something out of the corner of her eye. She glanced over her shoulder and saw that someone was standing there behind her. *The gardener,* she thought to herself, too confused from sorrow and fear to make sense out of anything that was happening.

" 'Why are you crying? Who are you looking for?' the man asked.

"Thinking that she was talking to the gardener, she said, 'Please, if you have taken Him, tell me where you've put Him.'

" 'Mary!'

"As soon as He said her name, she recognized Jesus. She let out a yell of excitement. 'You're back! I have You back!'

"He told her gently, 'You can't keep Me, though, Mary, not like this. I have to go up to my Father before too long. And I need you to go tell the others that I am alive. Tell them that I will be going up to my Father soon. But remember—My Father is your Father, and My God is your God.'

"So Mary ran and found us and gave us the Lord's message.

"That evening we were all together with the doors locked tight in case the Jewish leaders should find us, and suddenly Jesus was standing there with us. 'Peace to you,' He said, and we heard the joy and love in His voice.

"As He spoke, He held out His hands, so we could see

the scars the nails had left in His palms. Then He showed us the place on His side where the soldier had stuck the spear into Him, and we knew for sure that He was really Jesus, our Master. I began to laugh out loud, with tears running down my face. I felt as though I had just woken up from the worst nightmare I had ever had—only to find that a bright and glorious morning had dawned.

"We all gathered around Him. And then He said one of those funny things that took us by surprise again, the way He always did. 'If you forgive anyone's sins,' He said, 'they are forgiven.'

"Peter and I glanced at each other. I was remembering the way I had raced ahead of him that morning, determined to get to the grave first—and I guess he was thinking of the way he had pushed past me to get inside the tomb. We gave each other a couple of sheepish grins, and then we hugged each other. We knew that even something little like that had to be forgiven. We couldn't stand in the presence of our risen Lord knowing that anything was between us.

"The next forty days were wonderful. Now at last we were finally beginning to understand what Jesus had been trying to teach us all along. He wasn't going to set up an earthly kingdom, with thrones and rulers and important people to help the king. Instead, He was the King of a different sort of realm, a kingdom of love and forgiveness that would last forever.

"Still, a few of us kept thinking that He would set up the other sort of kingdom while He was at it. We kept asking Him if now He was going to free our country from the Roman emperor.

" 'God decides when those sort of things will happen,' He told us. 'Don't worry about all that. When the Holy Spirit has come upon you, you will receive power to tell everyone about Me, all over the world.'

"Soon after that, when we were all together one day, Jesus disappeared from our sight—He went up into the sky. Just as He had told Mary Magdalene, He went back to His Father, and we no longer have His physical presence here with us on earth. But He sent us His Spirit. He is in our hearts now, and nothing can ever separate us from His love. And that is the miracle that happens to each of us."

CHAPTER 7

"Do you understand now?" Aaron asked Rachel.

She sucked in a deep breath, her eyes on John's face. "That really happened?" she asked the old man. "Just the way you said?"

He nodded, and she could read the truth in his gaze. "I saw it all with my own eyes."

Rachel rubbed her eyes with her fists, suddenly as exhausted as if she had worked hard all day, instead of sitting here listening to an old man talk. "I'm not sure," she said slowly. "I'm still not sure I understand."

"No," John said gently, "it is not easy to grasp the good news that Jesus brought us. And yet it is very simple. All we have to do is give our lives to Jesus—and in return He gives us Himself, the never-dying life."

Thoughtfully, Rachel watched an ant crawl across her bare foot. She thought about her father, and how sad she and her mother had been ever since he died. "You really think when we die—when our bodies die, I mean—that we will still be alive with Jesus? Can Jesus really work a miracle like that? Even though we can't see Him?"

John nodded. "One time when Jesus was talking to us, He promised that His Father's house had many different kinds of mansions in it, wonderful homes for everyone, where we can all live forever. 'If it weren't true,' He said, 'I would have told you.' Believe me, Rachel, the Master always spoke the truth. He wouldn't have let us go on believing something if it weren't true. That's why He worked so many miracles. He wanted us to understand the real truth about His kingdom, a truth that will last forever."

Rachel thought about a wonderful mansion where she could live with her parents in Jesus' kingdom—and then she remembered the small, dark house she shared with her mother. She sighed; she needed to get home and do her chores. Her mother would be coming back soon, tired from her long day gleaning grain. They would have a little wheat to make bread, but her mother would be too hungry to wait, and Rachel had never gotten to the market. She felt tired and sad for a moment, remembering how dark and dreary her life with her mother was since her father had died. But maybe. . .maybe if what the old man said was true, then none of that mattered quite so much. If she were part of Jesus' kingdom, then His love and life were everywhere. Maybe she could even find them in the cramped, dirty house that was her home now. . . .

She got to her feet. "I need to go," she told John. She felt suddenly shy, and she hesitated, wanting to say something more, but not certain how to say it. "Thank you," she said at last, her voice soft and gruff. "Thank you for telling me about Jesus' miracles."

John smiled. "You are welcome, anytime. I like nothing better than to talk about the Master. But wait a moment, Child." He pushed himself up from the bench. "Let me get you a basket of food to take home to your mother. I have more than I can ever eat, and it would be a shame for it to go to waste."

Rachel skipped up the narrow street that led to her house, her mind busy. If she gave her life to Jesus, the way the old man had said, would Jesus really fill her with His life and love? Would John turn out to have spoken the truth about Jesus and His miracles? The basket that hung from her arm distracted her from her thoughts for a moment. It was so heavy that she could hardly wait to show it to her mother. They would have enough food for the entire week, and that in itself seemed like a miracle to her. Now she would have to hurry and do her chores before her mother got back. . . .

When she ducked through the door, though, she found that her mother was already there, sitting slumped on the floor, her face pale in the shadows.

"I'll get busy now, Mother," Rachel said in a rush. "But look what I've brought you." She held out the basket.

Her mother got to her feet, but she ignored the basket of food. She stepped close to Rachel and looked into her face.

"Child," she said slowly, "I can't remember the last time

you didn't have a frown on your face." She touched her daughter's cheek with her hand. "But you're smiling!" She took a deep breath and let out a little laugh. "Oh, Rachel. It's a miracle!"

THE PARABLES OF JESUS

by Ellyn Sanna

CHAPTER 1

"I hate the Romans!" Twelve-year-old Zadok watched the soldiers march by and scowled. "When will Jesus make them go away? When will He set up His kingdom?" He looked up at his father as they walked home from the harbor where they had left their fishing boat. Soon, he hoped his father would say. Next week. Tomorrow. . .

But instead his father only sighed and shrugged his shoulders. "I don't know, Son."

Simon, Zadok's father, was a Zealot, a member of the rebel group that hoped to drive the Romans out of Israel. The Zealots believed the Romans had no right to rule God's people. They hated the Roman taxes, and when the Romans took a census of all the people who lived in the land, the Zealots refused to be counted. Zadok had grown up hearing his father talk with the other Zealots, and over the years, he, too, had come to hate these foreigners who ruled their country.

The Zealots also worshiped God and read the Torah, and Zadok had once loved to hear his father read to him from the Scriptures. Lately, though, Zadok thought less and less about loving God, and more and more about hating the Romans. He and his father worked hard on their fishing boat—

but too much of the money they earned for their catch went to pay the Roman taxes. *It's not fair,* Zadok thought to himself as he scuffed his feet along the dusty street. They should overthrow the Romans now, before the Romans took one more coin from their pockets. Zadok wouldn't be afraid to take up a sword and fight. . . .

His father walked thoughtfully beside him, his gaze on the green hills behind their village. A few months ago, Simon had become a disciple of Jesus of Nazareth, the new rabbi who claimed to be the Messiah, the one who would free their land. Zadok was filled with excitement whenever he thought of Jesus.

As they reached their home, Zadok tugged at his father's robe. "When you were with Him yesterday, did Jesus mention His kingdom?" he asked.

His father washed his hands and then settled himself at the table. He waited until Zadok's mother Lydia brought the last dish of food from the oven, and then, when they were all ready, he asked the blessing for their meal. Breaking off a hunk of bread to dip in his stew, he turned to Zadok. "Yes, Jesus did speak of His kingdom yesterday. But first He told us a story."

Zadok gulped down a chunk of meat. "Tell me what He said."

"All right," Simon answered. "Here is how the parable

of the sower went. . . .

"Once there was a farmer, who was getting ready for the spring planting, just like all the other farmers. He took a big bag of seeds and hung it around his neck, and then he went out into his fields. Now he would plant his seeds, so that when they grew and ripened, he would have plenty of crops to harvest. As he walked through his fields, he scooped out handfuls of seed and tossed them from side to side across the dirt.

"Unfortunately, not all of the seeds fell on soft earth. Instead, some landed on the farmer's footpath. The ground there was hard and packed, not loose and soft like the plowed soil, and the seeds just lay there, not doing anything. Eventually, some birds came and gobbled them up.

"Meanwhile, the farmer kept on tossing his seeds from side to side as he walked along. And some of the seeds fell on rock that was covered with only a few inches of soil. Over the next few days, these seeds germinated and little plants quickly sprang up. But of course they did not last long. Their roots had nowhere to grow, so when the sun grew hot, they could not draw up any moisture from the earth. In the end, they wilted and died.

"But the farmer still tossed his seeds from side to side. Some of it fell on ground that was choked with weeds and thorns. The seeds tried to grow there, but before long the stronger growth pushed out the young shoots.

"The farmer still kept on throwing his seeds onto the ground. And some of it fell on soft, fertile soil. These seeds germinated and sank their roots deep into the earth. They grew tall and strong—and before long they produced a crop so enormous that it was thirty, no, sixty, no, even one hundred times as great as the number of seeds the farmer had originally planted."

Zadok wrinkled his forehead. "That was a strange story," he said slowly. He was trying to remember the farmers he had seen in the spring planting their crops in the fields outside town. Something about Jesus' story didn't seem quite right. "Why would a farmer plant his seeds that way? Don't farmers usually plow out the stones and weeds first, before they plant? They don't just throw their seeds up in the air like that, do they?"

His father smiled and shook his head. "No, most farmers don't act like the farmer in Jesus' story. But any farmer I know would be delighted if even some of his seeds produced thirty times as much harvest, let alone one hundred times as much. I don't know of any farmer whose fields yield more than ten times as much crops as seeds." Simon took a last bite of bread, then wiped a few drops of stew from his beard.

Zadok reached for the bowl of figs at the center of the table. He was trying to puzzle out the story's meaning. What had Jesus been trying to say? "So this wasn't meant to be a true story then?"

His father shook his head. "No, not true in the sense that Jesus was talking about an actual farmer planting his fields. But it was true in another sense."

"What do you mean?" Zadok took a bite of the fig.

"Well," his father answered, "when Jesus finished His story, He said, 'If you are willing to hear, then listen and understand.' I think He told us a story to give us a picture of what He was trying to tell us, a picture that would stick in our heads better than a long sermon. We could take that picture with us, and maybe we will spend the rest of our lives looking at it, thinking it over, understanding more and more what it means."

Zadok's mother stood up and began clearing the table. "And just what do you think Jesus' story meant?" she asked her husband.

He leaned back from the table. "I'll tell you how Jesus explained it to us."

"When the seed fell on the path," Simon began, recalling Jesus' words, "where the dirt was hard and packed, that is like when someone hears the good news about God's kingdom, but they don't understand what they are hearing. God's good news can't take root in their lives, and soon the Evil One comes and snatches the seed out of their hearts. The seed might as well never have fallen on their hearts for all the good it does. It didn't change them even one little bit.

"The soil that was thin and rocky is like people who are delighted to hear about God's kingdom—but their roots are too shallow for them to truly grow. They are happy enough at first, but as soon as they begin to have any kind of troubles or sadness, then their new life begins to droop. Pretty soon that life dies altogether.

"The seeds that were choked out by weeds and thorns are like people who do hear and accept the good news from God —but before you know it, they are so worried about their problems and so busy taking care of their lives, trying to get themselves the things they want, they forget all about God. Of course, those seeds will never have any fruit, because they just can't get enough nourishment. All these people's energy goes toward making others think they are important or getting lots of things or having fun. Those things take up their whole lives. They just don't have anything left for God's kingdom.

"But the good soil, the soil that is soft and rich, is like those people who open their hearts to God's message. And when they do, they grow so much that their lives make an unbelievable amount of fruit, more fruit than makes sense by ordinary standards. That's because the seed that God grows in our lives is amazing, spectacular, miraculous."

That night as Zadok sat in front of the fire, he found himself thinking again about the story Jesus had told. He wanted to have room in his heart for the good news that Jesus talked about—but he wasn't sure what that meant. If the Romans were gone, that would be good news. Did Jesus mean that setting up the Jewish kingdom should be more important than anything else? That made sense; that's what all the Zealots said, too.

Or did Jesus mean something different? Zadok wondered. He looked at his parents as they murmured the evening prayers, and he thought to himself that they must be like the good soil. They were always praying and talking about God.

But did he, Zadok, have good soil in his heart? Sometimes lately he felt so confused and angry. Was his heart so hard that he would never be changed at all by the things Jesus said? Or was he so shallow that these new seeds would have no room to send down deep roots? He found his thoughts wandering, and he sighed, realizing that his thoughts were quite weedy a lot of the time.

Zadok turned to look at his father, who had picked up some fishing nets to mend. "Why doesn't Jesus gather an army if the kingdom of God is so important to Him?"

His father's fingers moved quickly, tying the cord in strong knots that would hold the weight of many fish. After a moment, he looked up at his son. "I'm not sure I know.

But let me tell you another story Jesus told us."

"Jesus told a parable of the wheat and weeds," Simon began. "It went like this:

"The kingdom of heaven is like a farmer who planted his field full of good, healthy wheat seeds. He went to bed tired out but happy, knowing he had done his job well, and that the wheat was all safely planted in the rich, moist earth.

"But this farmer had an enemy, and that enemy played a mean trick on him. While the farmer was sleeping, his enemy came creeping through the darkness, a bag full of weed seeds over his shoulder. Quietly, the enemy planted those weed seeds right in the same field with the good wheat seed the farmer had just planted. And then the enemy crept back home, without anyone ever knowing the mischief he had done.

"But as the farmer's wheat germinated and began to send up little green shoots, so did the enemy's weeds. Pretty soon, anyone who walked by the field could plainly see that it was full of both wheat and weeds. So the farmer's servants decided they had better let the farmer know he had a problem.

" 'Sir,' they said, 'you know that field where you planted the wheat?'

"The farmer looked up and nodded.

" 'Well. . .' The servants bit their lips, wondering how to tell the farmer their bad news. Finally, one of them blurted, 'The field is full of weeds!'

"The farmer frowned. When he planted the wheat, he was sure all the weeds had been pulled out of the field—so how could it be full of weeds now? Suddenly, he remembered his enemy who liked to play mean tricks. 'An enemy has done it!' he shouted.

"The servants looked surprised; they had assumed the weeds had gotten into the field in the usual, mysterious way that weeds always got into a field. They had never dreamed that an enemy might have sneaked in and planted weed seeds in with the wheat.

" 'So,' one of them asked, 'should we go pull out the weeds?' He sighed, thinking how much work it would be to weed the whole field. His knees hurt just thinking about it.

"But the farmer surprised them even more now. 'No,' he said, shaking his head. 'If you do that, you might hurt the young wheat plants—maybe even pull up the wrong plants by mistake. No, you might as well let both the weeds and wheat grow together for now. When harvesttime comes, then I will tell the harvesters to sort out the weeds from wheat. The wheat I will put into the barn, and the weeds I will throw away and burn.' "

Zadok leaned back on his hands, his eyes on the dancing

flames in front of him. "That's a funny story, too," he said thoughtfully. "You'd think that the farmer would have done something to save his wheat from the weeds. But instead he doesn't do anything. He doesn't even try to get even with his enemy. He just waits until the harvest." He turned away from the fire's heat and faced his father. "What do you think this story means?"

His father set aside his nets. "Well, Zadok, this is what Jesus told us when we were alone with Him later."

"Jesus is the farmer who plants the good wheat seed," Simon recalled, "and His field is the world. The wheat seed stands for the people who belong to His kingdom, and the weeds are those people who close their hearts to Jesus and choose to put themselves first. In real life, the enemy is the Devil, for he is the one who wants us to turn away from God's love and put ourselves ahead of anything else. Our harvest will come at the end of this world, and the harvesters are the angels.

"When the world ends, Jesus will finally send His angels, and they will pull out anything that makes people turn from God—and everyone who has chosen evil will be burned. These people will be in terrible pain; they will be sobbing and grinding their teeth. But the good seed, the people who opened their hearts to God, will be saved for eternity, where they will shine as bright as the sun."

Zadok frowned. "Why does Jesus talk so much about

love? Doesn't He hate the Romans? Does He expect us to wait for the angels to free us?" He yawned, suddenly sleepy. "I don't understand why God doesn't just take all the evil out of the world right now, instead of sitting back and waiting for the end of the world."

His father nodded. "Some things are hard to understand." He looked up at Zadok's mother as she got to her feet.

"Time for bed, Zadok," she said.

Zadok nodded, but he waited a moment longer to hear if his father had anything more to say that would help him understand.

Simon sighed. "I get discouraged sometimes when I hear all the rumors about the bad things happening in our world. We Jews have little hope against Rome if we are not united—but I am afraid the Jewish leaders will never accept Jesus. I wonder where all the anger and bitterness will end. I fear something terrible will happen, something truly evil. . . ." He sighed again. "But Jesus told us something else today about His kingdom, something that encourages me."

His wife put her hand on his shoulder. "What did He say, Simon?"

Simon gazed into the fire, his eyes thoughtful. "He said that His kingdom is like a mustard seed. You know how tiny that is, barely more than a speck. And yet from that tiny seed grows a tall plant, a plant that is as tall as a tree, a plant where all the birds can come and roost when they're tired." Simon smiled. "I guess when all we can see is little specks of God's kingdom, scattered here and there through our lives, we just have to trust that a tall, strong plant will one day grow from those tiny seeds."

As Zadok settled himself on his sleeping mat, he was still frowning. He knew God's kingdom still existed, in spite of the Romans, but he didn't know how to look for those tiny seeds his father had mentioned.

Seeds! he thought grumpily to himself. *What does a kingdom have to do with seeds?*

CHAPTER 2

Zadok's father was gone for several weeks, traveling with Jesus. While he was gone, Zadok thought about all Simon had said about the kingdom of God. Zadok wondered if Jesus would think that he, Zadok, deserved to be a part of God's kingdom—or would He think Zadok was a weed that needed to be burned? The thought made him uneasy, and he was anxious for his father to come home. Maybe when he did, he would be able to explain a little more about the kingdom Jesus would build once the Romans were gone.

At last, one afternoon when he and his mother were just sitting down to their noon meal, they heard a commotion out in the courtyard. Zadok hurried to the door and saw their donkey tied in his old place—and there was his father coming toward him! Zadok and his mother rushed at Simon with their arms open.

When they had all sat down and eaten, Zadok leaned toward his father. "So did you find out any more about God's kingdom? Will Jesus be setting up His kingdom soon, do you think? Will He get rid of all the Romans? Has He begun to build an army at last?"

Simon shook his head. "No, somehow I can't see Jesus leading an army. I don't think He will be that sort of king,

Son. Not a warrior."

"Oh." Zadok was disappointed. He loved hearing the old stories of the warlike Maccabees and the even older stories of Joshua. "Then what sort of king will He be? How can He get rid of the Romans without an army?"

Simon stretched his long legs, then patted his full stomach, smiling across the table at his wife. "I'm still not certain what kind of king Jesus will be. I'm not even sure I understand what His kingdom is like. He talks more about forgiving our enemies than about conquering them."

Zadok frowned. How could God want them to forgive the Romans for taking their land? Didn't God want His people to rule their own country again? "Did He tell you any more about His kingdom?" he asked eagerly.

Simon nodded. "Yes. I'm just not sure I understand. He keeps talking about the kingdom of heaven."

"Did He tell you another story?"

"Yes. He uses a lot of stories to teach us." His father settled himself more comfortably, then pulled Zadok's mother down beside him. "Let me tell you," he said, as he related Jesus' parable of the unforgiving debtor.

"The kingdom of heaven is like a king who had loaned money to his people. One day, he decided he should bring his accounts up to date, so he made appointments to meet with all the people who owed him money.

"Well, the first person he met with owed him millions of dollars. But when the king asked him where the money was, the fellow just shrugged. 'I'm sorry, Sir. I don't have it.' He hung his head then, looking worried. 'There's no way I'll ever be able to pay you back,' he whispered.

"The king slammed his fist down on the arm of his throne. 'That's it! You've had all this time to pay me, and you haven't even tried to get the money back to me. I've had it with you!' He turned to one of his servants. 'Take this man and sell him to someone who wants a slave. Take his wife and his children and sell them, too. Sell everything he owns as well, his house and everything in it.' The king shook his head grimly. 'One way or another, I'm going to get my money back.'

"The man who owed the millions of dollars buried his face in his hands and began to cry. 'Oh, please, Your Highness.' He threw himself down on the floor in front of the king's throne. 'Please, please,' he begged. 'Be patient with me! I will pay you back, just give me a little more time.'

"The king looked down at the man's shaking shoulders, and his face softened. He was too sorry for the man to be angry anymore. 'All right,' he said. 'You may go.'

"The man raised his head and peeked at the king between his fingers. 'You mean—?'

"The king waved his hand at him. 'Yes, yes, you're free to go. I won't sell you or your wife or your children or your house.'

" 'Oh, thank you, thank you, Your Highness,' the man cried. He scrambled to his feet and rushed to kiss the king's hand. 'You won't regret this, I promise you. I'll get your money to you as soon as I can. I should be able to get it by—'

"But the king interrupted him before he could finish. 'Oh, forget the debt. I've erased the whole thing. As of this moment, you don't owe me a cent.'

"The man could hardly believe his ears. He left the palace humming and skipping.

"But as he was on his way home, he passed a friend of his who owed him a couple thousand dollars, and suddenly he stopped singing and he stopped skipping. His friend was part of the reason why he had gotten into trouble with the king in the first place. *Why, if I hadn't loaned my friend that money, I would have been able to make my payments to the king,* he thought.

"The man was filled with frustration and resentment. He reached out and grabbed his friend by the throat. 'Just where do you think you're sneaking off to?' he growled. 'Did you think I wouldn't notice you?'

" 'N–n–no,' the other man stammered. 'I was just—'

" 'Don't try to give me any excuses!' the first man shouted. 'I'm sick of hearing you whine. I want my money, and I want it now.'

"His friend turned pale. 'Please,' he whispered, 'give me a little more time. I don't have the money right now, but I'll get it for you, if you'll just be patient. My wife has been sick, you know, and my cow died, and. . .'

"The first man squeezed his friend's throat a little tighter. 'I told you, I don't want to hear your feeble excuses. I'm calling the police to arrest you and throw you into jail. And you'll stay there until you give me my money!'

"And that is exactly what the first man did. He had his friend thrown into debtors' prison. But when people heard what he had done, they were upset, and some of them went to the king and told him what had happened.

"The king could hardly believe his ears when he heard what the man had done. Right away, he sent for him. 'You evil person!' he cried when the man came into the room. 'After I erased your debt, why couldn't you erase your friend's? You owed me millions of dollars, a far greater debt than your friend owed you. But I forgave you. So why didn't you forgive your friend?'

"The king shook his head in disappointment. And then he threw the man into debtors' prison until he could pay every penny of those millions of dollars he owed."

Lydia laughed as Simon finished the story. "I like that story."

Her husband turned to look at her. "Do you understand what Jesus meant?"

"Of course," she said, smiling. "It's perfectly clear. We all owe God more than we could ever pay Him—and yet He cancels our debts. He loves us and pities us. So when God has treated us with so much mercy, we ought to forgive each other for the much smaller debts we owe one another. Instead of keeping a list of all the wrongs done to us, figuring out exactly how people ought to be treating us to repay all that we've done for them, we should just erase all our lists. Rip them into pieces. How dare we not forgive each other when God has forgiven us?"

Zadok frowned at his mother. "But what has that got to do with God's kingdom?"

His mother stood up and began clearing the table. "Well, it certainly is a very different kingdom than any I've ever heard of. I suspect it's a kingdom that wouldn't fight many wars, at least not the sort with spears and swords." She glanced at her son's disappointed face and laughed, but then she sobered. "Personally, that sounds good to me, Zadok. I'm not in any hurry to have either you or your father going off to fight Romans. I would hate to have you shed anyone's blood. And I would hate even more to have you be wounded—or killed."

She looked from her son's face to her husband's. "When we can't forgive," she said softly, "then we are in prison. We're imprisoned inside our own hearts. Just like the two of you. You hate the Romans so much that I wonder sometimes if either of you will ever be really free."

Zadok rolled his eyes. "Why would God want us to forgive the Romans, Mother? He must hate them as much as we do." He turned to his father. "Jesus must have meant that we should forgive each other, our own people. The Romans aren't a part of His kingdom. Right?"

His father scratched his beard. "I don't know, Son," he said after a moment. "I don't know." He sighed. "Let me tell you another story Jesus told us while we were gone." He glanced at his wife and smiled. "We'll see if your mother can make sense of this one."

So Simon began telling Jesus' parable of the vineyard workers.

"The kingdom of heaven is like a rich landowner who owned a huge vineyard. The grapes in his vineyard were ready to be picked, so he got up at daybreak and hired some people to harvest the grapes. He discussed with the workers how much he would pay them, and they soon settled on a fair price for a day's wages.

"Later in the morning, while walking through the marketplace the landlord noticed some people standing around doing nothing. 'Hey, you!' he called to them. 'Would you like a chance to earn some money?'

"The people agreed that they would be happy to make some money.

" 'Good, good!' the landowner said, clapping his hands. 'Go on up to my vineyard and get picking. At the end of the day, I'll pay you whatever is fair.'

"So the people made their way to his vineyard and got to work.

"The landowner went on his way happily, but then he noticed gray clouds building up in the sky, and he worried that rain might rot his wonderful grape harvest. So at noon he went back to the marketplace and hired more workers to pick the grapes. The rain held off, but just in case, he hired even more workers again at three o'clock in the afternoon.

"At about five o'clock that evening, he happened to be in town again, and he noticed another group of people standing around doing nothing. 'Hey!' he called to them. 'Why haven't you been working today?'

"They looked at him in surprise. 'Because no one hired us,' one of them told him.

" 'Well, I'll hire you,' the landowner said. 'Go on up and get to work with the others in my vineyard.'

"When night fell, all the grapes were picked at last. The landowner told his foremen to call in the workers and give them their day's wages, beginning with the last workers first. To everyone's surprise, those hired at five o'clock got a full day's wages. The workers who had been hired earlier in the day nudged each other, and their faces lit up. 'If those guys got all that for just an hour's work,' they whispered, 'just think what we'll get!'

"But when their turn came, they found that their pay was the same as the first group's. 'That's not fair!' they all cried. The ones who had been working since daybreak were especially angry. 'You paid them just as much for one hour of work as you did us who worked all day in the scorching heat. It's not fair!'

"The landowner just smiled at them. 'Friends,' he said, 'I haven't been unfair. Didn't we agree this morning on a fair price for a day's work? Well, here it is. So take it and be happy. If I want to pay the last workers as much as the first, why is that any of your business? You have what belongs to you, and I can do whatever I want with my money. Why are you angry with me for being kind to these people? How does that hurt you in any way?' "

Zadok's mother sat down beside Simon and reached for her mending. "Doesn't that sound just like Zadok and his cousins?" she laughed. " 'It's not fair,' they always say. When I'm handing out the raisins or the sweetbread, those boys are so worried about who gets what, they hardly enjoy what they have in their hand." She chuckled. "This Jesus of yours knows human nature, Simon."

Her husband nodded. "Yes, He does. But why do you suppose He keeps saying that the kingdom is like a person? His stories never quite make sense."

His wife took a few stitches, her face thoughtful. "I don't know," she said at last. "I don't understand, either. But that last story sounds as though we may all be surprised to find out just who belongs to God's kingdom in the end. We may find we are sharing the kingdom with people we never suspected would be there."

"Not Romans," Zadok said flatly, his face stormy.

"Who knows?" his mother asked lightly. "You might be surprised."

"But that doesn't make any sense," he protested. "They are the ones who took our kingdom from us. We can't share our land with them. We have to drive them out. How else can our land belong to God again instead of the Roman emperor?"

His mother shrugged her shoulders. "I don't know. But I wonder sometimes if our own leaders belong to God's kingdom any more than the Romans do."

Simon nodded, his face sober. "I think Jesus would agree with you there. You should have heard Him the last time we were at the temple. He told a story the Jewish leaders didn't like too well, I can tell you."

Zadok's mother laid down her sewing. "Tell us," she said quietly.

"Jesus told the parable of the evil farmers," Simon began.

"Once upon a time, there was a rich landowner who

decided he would grow grapes on his property. So he planted the grapevines, and then he built a wall around the vineyard, to keep out the animals and thieves. Next, he dug a pit for pressing the juice out of the grapes, and last of all he built a lookout tower so that guards could keep watch over his land.

"When all that was finished, he leased the vineyard to tenant farmers and moved to another country. But when the time came for the grape harvest to be ready, he sent some of his servants back to collect his share of the crop.

"Meanwhile, though, the tenant farmers had been wishing they could keep all the crop for themselves. They were hoping the landowner would never come back at all, so they could take over the vineyard completely. Needless to say, they weren't very happy when they saw the landowner's servants come walking in. In fact, they were so angry, they grabbed the servants and attacked them. They beat one of them, they threw stones at another, and they even killed one of them.

"When the landowner did not hear anything from his servants, he became worried. This time he sent a larger group of servants to collect his share of the crop, but the evil tenant farmers treated these people the same way they had the first group. Finally, the landowner decided to send his own son, whom he loved very much. 'They at least ought to respect him,' he said to himself.

"But when the farmers saw the son coming, they laughed out loud and nudged each other with their elbows. 'Here comes the landowner's heir,' they muttered to each other. 'If we kill him, there will be no one left to inherit the land—and we can keep the estate for ourselves! Come on!' And they grabbed the landowner's son and dragged him outside the vineyard. There they murdered him.

"When the owner of the vineyard returns to his land, what do you think he will do?"

"Well," said Zadok's mother quietly, her hands in her lap, "I hope the Jewish leaders didn't hear that story."

"Oh, they heard it," Simon said grimly. "And they were not happy at all. I heard rumors that they wanted to arrest Jesus after that story—but they were afraid to, because He's so popular with the crowds."

Zadok scratched his nose. "Did Jesus just end the story with a question like that?"

His father nodded. "Yes, He did."

"But what does it mean?" Zadok asked. "What was Jesus talking about?"

Simon leaned back. "I think, Son, that Jesus was saying that the Jews have refused to listen to God's prophets—so God sent His Son to us. But if the Jews refuse to acknowledge Him as well, then I fear for what will happen. Maybe the landowner will take the vineyard away from the farmers and let other people tend the grapes instead."

"Do you mean. . . ?" Zadok struggled to make sense out of his father's words. "Do you really think that God would give His kingdom to someone else besides the Jews?"

Simon shook his head. "I don't know, Son," he said heavily. "I just don't know."

Zadok was silent for a moment, thinking. "But we have listened to the prophets," he burst out at last. "Just because the Pharisees and the priests are bad, that doesn't mean we all are."

"No," Simon agreed. He smiled at his son. "And I do not believe Jesus would shut any of His true followers out of His kingdom."

Zadok put his chin in his hands, thinking some more about Jesus' story. One little piece of the story puzzled him especially, and after a moment, he lifted his head and looked at his father. "Is Jesus really God's Son? Not just a prophet, the way we thought—I guess that would be like one of the servants the landowner sent. Do you think He is God's actual Son?" The thought was mind-boggling.

A curious smile lit his father's face. "I'm not sure, Son. I still don't understand Jesus much better than you do. All I know is this: He's like no one I've ever known before." Simon put his hand on Zadok's shoulder. "I guess we'll just have to wait and see."

Zadok frowned. "Well, I still don't understand exactly

what Jesus thinks we should be doing to get ready for His kingdom. You'd think that even if He's as mad at the Jewish leaders as He is the Romans, He would still want us to figure out how to get rid of them. What good do all these stories do? We ought to be doing something. Does He want us just to wait around doing nothing?"

Simon shook his head. "No," he said slowly, "I don't think He wants us to do nothing. I get the feeling He expects us to get busy now."

Zadok shook his head in frustration. "But what are we supposed to be doing? I don't understand."

His mother gave a little laugh. "Seems to me Jesus has already made it pretty clear—He wants us to get busy forgiving our enemies."

Zadok made a face. "That's no way to set up a kingdom," he said stubbornly. "It doesn't make any sense."

"No," his father said, "it doesn't seem to. Sometimes Jesus talks as though God's kingdom is already right here, all around us, and all we have to do is step out and claim it. And other times He talks as though we shouldn't be surprised if we have to wait a long time before we see the reign of God here on earth. And then other times He speaks as though both are true at the same time." Simon shook his head. "He talks in riddles. But one thing is clear—He expects us to be working for the kingdom now. If you listen to one more of Jesus' stories, you'll see what I mean.

"Jesus told a parable of talents," Simon recalled, then began quoting His words.

"The kingdom of heaven is like a rich man who was going on a trip. Before he left, he called his servants together and gave them each money to invest for him while he was gone. He had thought carefully about how much to give each servant, and he decided to base the amount on each person's abilities. He was a generous man, and he wanted to loan them an enormous amount of his wealth, so in the end he gave one of his servants as much money as the servant normally could have earned in one hundred years of work, five big bags of gold. Another servant received as much money as he could have earned in forty years of work, two big bags of gold. The last servant received twenty years' worth of gold, a big bag filled to the top.

"As soon as the rich man had gone on his trip, the servant with five bags of gold went out and got busy. He invested his gold, and before long he had doubled it. The servant with two bags of gold also went to work right away, and before long he, too, had doubled his money. But the servant who had only one bag of gold was afraid to use it. So he dug a hole in the ground, and he hid the rich man's money.

"After a long time, the rich man came back from his trip. He called in his servants to see how they had made out with the wealth he had loaned them. When the first two servants told him they had doubled the money he had given them, he was delighted. 'Well done!' he cried. 'You are good and faithful servants. And since you have done so well with this small amount I loaned you, now I want to give you still more. You will be responsible for an even greater part of my wealth, because you did so well with this.' He clapped the two men on the shoulders, and he spoke to them not as though they were servants, but as though he suddenly looked at them as dear friends. 'And now,' he cried, 'let's throw a party to celebrate your hard work!'

"Then he turned to the last servant. 'How did you make out?' the rich man asked him.

"The servant shuffled his feet, wondering if maybe he should have been more daring like his fellow servants. 'Well,' he said, giving his master an uneasy smile, 'I know what a hard deal you drive, Sir. And I knew you wouldn't have liked it if I lost what you gave me. So I dug a hole and buried the gold. I was scared, you see, Sir. But here it is!'

"The rich man's face grew dark. 'You lazy man! My wealth can accomplish absolutely nothing if it's hidden away in the ground.' He sighed in exasperation. 'Here, give your bag of gold to this person who has ten bags of gold. Those who use well what they are given end up with even more, for I have abundant wealth to share. But those who are not faithful to me with a little bit of wealth, will lose even that.'

He turned away from the servant in disgust. 'Throw him out!' he said over his shoulder to the other servants. 'He doesn't belong in my home.' "

Zadok hit his fist against his knee in frustration. "What does this story have to do with establishing God's kingdom? I don't understand. What wealth has God given us that we should be using for Him?"

His mother put a gentle hand on his arm, calming him. "God has given us much wealth, Son."

Zadok looked around their small house. "I don't see any," he said bitterly. "The Romans get it all."

His mother shook her head. "I see wealth the Romans cannot touch." She smiled. "I see a family who has much love to share, both with each other and with those outside. I see three healthy bodies that have great strength for serving God and those around us. I see three pairs of hands for reaching out to those who ask for help, three pairs of feet for carrying kindness to those in need, three mouths able to speak words of love and forgiveness to all those around us. I see three pairs of eyes that see the beauty of God's world —and three hearts that can open themselves to God's presence in our lives. That is great wealth indeed, my son."

Zadok shook his head, but he bit his tongue against the angry words that threatened to spill out of his mouth.

Simon leaned forward and looked into his wife's face.

"Did you hear this story from someone else before I told it to you?" he asked her.

She shook her head. "No. Why do you ask?"

"Because," her husband replied slowly, "after Jesus had told this story, He went on to say something very similar to what you just said."

Lydia's face lit with interest. "What did He say?"

"He said. . ." Simon squinted his eyes, trying to remember Jesus' exact words. "He said that when we do something very simple for another, something like giving food to someone who is hungry, or water to someone who is thirsty, then we are really doing it for the Ruler of God's kingdom. If we give clothing to a poor person, Jesus said, or take care of someone who is sick, or visit someone in prison, or welcome a stranger into our home, then we do it for the King. And if we refuse to do these things, then we are actually refusing to serve our King."

A look of delight crossed Lydia's face, but Zadok still scowled, trying to puzzle out the meaning of Jesus' words. "Does Jesus mean that God is the King?" he asked his father.

His father sat back, a thoughtful look on his face. "I think," he said, "that Jesus is the King."

Zadok felt a flicker of relief. Jesus was a flesh-and-blood man, and if He claimed to be the King, then sooner or later He would have to set up His kingdom—and that meant the Romans would have to be overthrown. He gave a grim smile.

But his mother shook her head at his expression. "Think, Son, what it will mean if Jesus is the Son of God. I'm not sure we can even imagine the sort of kingdom He will rule."

Zadok was busy the next few days, helping his father on his fishing boat. After being gone so many days with Jesus, Simon was eager to bring in a catch big enough to earn the gold he would need to keep his family fed. While they worked together, father and son spoke often about Jesus, but Zadok noticed that his father no longer seemed as frustrated with the Romans as he once had. He seemed less angry, gentler, more thoughtful; and his new attitude disturbed Zadok. *Maybe,* he thought, *Father would be better off if he stopped following Jesus.*

But a little voice kept interrupting Zadok's thoughts, bothering him. What if Jesus really was God's Son? What would that mean?

He tried to tell himself that if Jesus was God's actual Son, then He would have that much more power over the Romans. Even the Roman legions would never be able to resist a King who came from God. And yet Zadok was uneasy. He had a scared feeling in his stomach that things were changing somehow—and yet none of the changes were the ones he had looked for and hoped for.

After a particularly successful day of fishing, Simon left Zadok to clean down the boat and mend the sails, while he went to listen to more of Jesus' teaching. The next day as they set out to sea once more, Simon was unusually quiet. At last, Zadok asked him, "Did you find out any more about the kingdom?"

Simon's eyes lingered on the horizon for a long moment, and then he nodded. "Yes, Jesus told us more stories about His kingdom. I think it's clear now that He is not talking about a kingdom for Jews only."

Zadok's lips pressed tightly together, biting back his disappointment. But then a new thought occurred to him. *Does Jesus want all the nations ruled now by the Romans to rise up together? To form a united rebellion against Rome?* The thought sent a thrill of excitement through him.

"Tell me," he said. "Tell me what Jesus said."

"Well," Simon began, "Jesus told a parable of a wedding feast. It went something like this.

"The kingdom of heaven is like a king who prepares a great feast to celebrate the wedding of his son. The king is overflowing with joy, and he longs to share his delight with the people of his kingdom. He eagerly awaits the wedding day.

"When everything is ready, he sends his servants to tell everyone to come to the party. To his great disappointment, though, the servants come back alone.

" 'No one wants to come,' they tell him. 'Everyone

refused your invitation.'

" 'There must have been some misunderstanding,' the king says. He calls to some other servants, thinking that these people will do a better job taking his wonderful message to his friends. 'Go on,' he tells these servants. 'Let everyone know that the party is ready to begin. Tell them about the food I have prepared. Tell them what a good time we're going to have. Tell them to hurry!'

"But this group of servants has even worse luck than the first group had. At first people simply ignore them, going about their business as usual, working on their farms and tending their stores. When the servants insist the people listen to the king's invitation, they are full of excuses.

'I have to go look at a field I just bought,' one of them says. 'I just got married myself,' another says, 'and my wife wants me at home.' 'I have to go look at some oxen,' yet another tells the king's servants. These are all such lame excuses that the king's messengers keep on asking them to come to the party, but then the people become angry with them. They attack the king's servants and beat them up, and they even kill some of them.

"When the king hears what has happened, he is furious. Now he sends out his army to destroy the murderers and burn their city. Then he turns to his servants again. 'I am ready to celebrate the wedding of my son. The food is on the table, and the party is set to begin. But the guests I invited aren't worthy of joining our joy. So this time, forget about the important people in my kingdom. This time go out to the street corners and the alleys, and ask everyone you see to come to my party. Bring the poor people, the blind, the people who are sick. Bring people who can't walk, people who have no friends, people who are out of work and discouraged.'

"So the servants hurry off to do what the king asked. When they come back, one of them goes to the king and says, 'Your Highness, we have done what you asked, but the tables still aren't full at the party. Would you like us to invite anyone else?'

"The king nods, and his eyes are bright with joy and love. 'Yes,' he says, 'go back again, but this time go out beyond the city into the country lanes. Invite everyone you see. And insist that I want them all, good and bad, poor and sick, everyone. I want them all to join us in our wedding celebration. I want my house to be full to the brim. But those people who refused my invitation will be left out; they won't even get a taste of the leftovers.' "

Zadok helped his father haul a net full of fishes onto the deck. But all the while he was sorting the gleaming, flopping fish, his mind was dwelling on Jesus' story.

At first he thought the story meant that his new theory was right: Jesus wanted to include in His kingdom the

Gentile nations that were also oppressed by Rome's empire. That made sense to Zadok, at least in a way. After all, they would be stronger if they all worked together. His mind wandered off, wondering how they could organize themselves. And how would they make sure that the land of Israel belonged to its people? Would Israel rule the other surrounding countries, the way Rome now did?

Zadok liked that thought—but something told him this way of thinking didn't fit in with all Jesus had said. *Why, Zadok wondered, does Jesus keep talking about poor people and sick people, people who can't see or walk?* Zadok felt sorry for people like that—but really, what good were sick, weak people when it came to setting up a kingdom? They couldn't fight. They couldn't really do much of anything, could they?

Zadok cast a sideways glance at his father, wondering what he was thinking. Before Simon became Jesus' disciple, he had shared everything with Zadok. Together father and son had plotted the overthrow of Rome, and Zadok had always loved to listen to his father talk with the other Zealots who were scheming against the Roman Empire. But now, sometimes Zadok wasn't sure what his father was thinking. Now that he was one of Jesus' disciples, Simon seldom met with his old Zealot friends. He was quieter than he used to be, and Zadok had the feeling he was lost in thought most of the time, pondering the stories he had heard from Jesus.

Zadok, suddenly filled with impatience, threw a tiny fish into the sea. "How much longer do we have to wait?" he burst out. "Jesus keeps talking about the kingdom—but when are we going to see it?"

His father looked down into his face. "I don't know, Son. The things Jesus told us last night make me wonder. Maybe we will have to be patient for a long time. Maybe the important thing is to be ready, whenever the kingdom finally does arrive."

Zadok's forehead wrinkled. "What do you mean?"

His father shrugged. "I'm not sure. Let me tell you another story that Jesus told us."

"Jesus said," Simon recalled, "that when the kingdom of heaven comes it will be like this:

"Once ten bridesmaids were waiting for the bridegroom to arrive at the wedding. The young women decided to take their lamps and go out to meet him. They would hold their oil lamps high like torches and line the road the wedding procession took on its way from the groom's house to the bride's. 'Won't our lamps look beautiful, burning in the darkness?' they asked each other as they hurried out to wait for the bridegroom to lead the bridal parade.

"Before they went too far, though, five of the young women stopped to think. 'What if the bridegroom is late?'

they asked themselves. 'Our oil will be all gone, and we'll have to stand there with unlit lamps. The wedding procession will have nothing to light its way, and our dark, empty lamps won't look beautiful at all.'

" 'Oh, come on,' the other five cried. 'Let's go. The bridegroom is sure to come soon. We don't want to bother with lugging along containers of oil with us. We might spill them on our pretty dresses.'

"But the first five bridesmaids shook their heads. 'You go on. We're going to bring extra oil with us, just in case. We'll catch up with you soon.' And they went back to get some containers of oil.

"They soon caught up with the other five bridesmaids, and together they waited for the bridegroom to lead the bridal party past them. But the hours went by, and still the bridegroom did not come. The bridesmaids began to yawn, and at last they curled up at the side of the road and went to sleep.

"At midnight a shout awakened them. 'The bridegroom is here! Come and meet him!'

"The ten bridesmaids sat up, rubbing their eyes. 'At last,' they grumbled. 'What kept him so long?'

"They reached for their lamps, so they could hold them high to light the road. But by now, of course, all the lamps had gone out. The five bridesmaids who had brought extra oil quickly poured it into their lamps, while the other five watched them sheepishly.

" 'Let us use some of your oil,' they said. 'Please?'

"But the first five bridesmaids shook their heads. 'We don't have enough for both our lamps and yours. If we give you oil, then our lamps will go out. No, you had better go to that shop on the corner and buy yourselves more oil.'

"Sighing, the second group of bridesmaids hurried off to the seller's oil shop. But while they were gone, the bridal procession came by, and by the time the bridesmaids got back from the shop, everyone had gone on to the bride's house for the wedding feast.

"They hurried to the house and pounded on the door. 'Let us in! Let us in!' they cried.

"The bridegroom came to the door, but he didn't open it. 'I don't know who you are,' he said. 'I can't open the door to strangers. Go away.'

"And the poor bridesmaids were left out in the dark and the cold, because they were not ready for the wedding."

Zadok scratched his head as his father finished talking. "I don't understand," he complained. "What is Jesus trying to say this time?"

Simon gazed out at the sea for a long moment. Then he sighed and turned toward his son. "I'm not sure, Zadok. But I think Jesus is calling us all to be ready for the kingdom right now. And at the same time, He is cautioning us that we must be prepared to wait. We have to do all that we can to get ready—today, this instant. But we must be willing to wait for as long as it takes." Simon stroked his beard, looking thoughtful. "It's as though Jesus is saying two things at once, the way He so often does. 'Hurry up and get ready,' He tells us on the one hand, and then on the other, He says, 'Be patient and wait.' "

Zadok wiped fish scales off his hands. "I don't want to wait any longer. I want the kingdom to come now."

"I know, Son." Simon's eyes lingered on his son's flushed face. "Zadok," he said slowly, "would you like to come with me tonight when I go to Jesus?"

Zadok's heart gave a funny jump inside his chest as he stared up into his father's face.

Simon smiled back at him. "The kingdom is so important to you, Zadok. I think it's time you heard Jesus for yourself."

Chapter 4

"Make sure you wash yourself good and clean," Zadok's mother urged him as she handed him a bucket of clean water. "I don't want you sitting at Jesus' feet smelling like a dead fish."

Zadok gave his mother a nervous grin as he took the water. He was excited that at last he would see Jesus for himself—but at the same time, his stomach was filled with nervous butterflies. What would Jesus think of him? Would Jesus answer his questions? He scrubbed his arms and face, and then ducked his whole head in the bucket of water. His hair dripping, he wiped his face with the towel his mother handed him and then scowled. "I don't know what the big fuss is all about," he muttered. "He's used to fishermen."

"He's the Son of God," Lydia breathed, her voice full of awe.

Goose bumps stood up on Zadok's arms, but then he pulled on a clean robe and turned away. From all that his father had told him, Jesus was an amazing leader. Zadok thought, however, *He couldn't really be the Son of God.*

Simon stuck his head in the archway that led from the street into their courtyard. "Ready?" he asked.

Zadok nodded.

"Don't keep him out too late, now," Lydia called to Simon.

Zadok rolled his eyes and hurried to catch up with Simon. "She still thinks I'm a child," he complained.

His father just laughed.

When they reached the house where Jesus was staying, they found a crowd had already gathered to hear Him speak. There were so many people that Jesus had come out into the street to talk to them; they would never have fit inside. Zadok was disappointed; he had hoped to be close enough to Jesus to ask Him questions. He and his father stood at the edge of the street, leaning against the wall, while Zadok tried to catch a glimpse of Jesus between all the heads.

Then Peter caught sight of Simon, and he grinned and motioned to him. "There's room for you and the boy up here," he called.

The crowd parted to make room for them, and Zadok found himself standing in front of a young bearded man in a tan robe. "This is my son, Master," he heard his father say. Simon put his hands on Zadok's shoulders and pushed him forward. "Zadok, this is the Master. This is Jesus."

Zadok looked up into the man's face. "Hello," he said shyly.

The brown eyes searched his face, and Zadok squirmed inside, wondering what the man was seeing. Then Jesus

smiled, and Zadok felt his heart leap. For a sudden, surprised moment, he felt as though he had just heard good
news, something amazing and wonderful and better than he
had ever hoped.

"I'm glad you are here, Zadok," Jesus said.

His voice was so gentle, that Zadok's eyes stung suddenly with tears. He blinked furiously. *How can a man
with a voice that soft be of any use as a leader?* he asked
himself.

Jesus smiled again, and one dark eyebrow raised. Zadok
flushed, wondering if Jesus had somehow guessed his
thoughts. He had so much he wanted to ask this man, but
his father was nudging him to one side, and he settled cross-
legged on the floor at Jesus' feet. He sucked in a deep breath,
looking sideways at Jesus from the corner of his eyes.

He looks pretty ordinary, Zadok decided, noticing Jesus'
worn sandals and plain robe. Jesus obviously didn't have
much money, and that might be a problem. After all, money
meant power, and they would need all the power they could
get if they were to overthrow the powerful Romans. Still,
money could be raised; the Zealots had often targeted the
rich men who were secretly sympathetic to their cause.

Zadok laughed to himself then, as he remembered Jesus'
claim to be the Son of God. Why would the Son of God
come to earth as a poor man? It made no sense, and he wondered if his father could have misunderstood Jesus' claim to

be the actual Son of God. For a person to claim to come from God like that, he would have to be either crazy—or evil, Zadok decided. He shivered, wondering if this man had somehow managed to totally mislead his father.

But then he darted a glance at Jesus' face. Jesus was laughing at something one of His disciples had said, and Zadok could see nothing in His expression that looked either crazy or bad. When Jesus glanced down and met Zadok's eyes, Zadok's face grew hot; he looked away quickly, his heart pounding. Something in Jesus' gaze made him feel different than he ever had before.

Jesus raised His hand then, and the crowd grew silent as He began to speak. "I tell you, friends, don't be scared of those who threaten to hurt you. All they can do is kill your body—but they have no power to do anything worse to you after that."

His voice was firm and loud, and Zadok was surprised at its power. He smiled to himself. Maybe this man would make a fearless leader, after all. *And these are good words to start off with,* Zadok thought, *words that will inspire the crowd to fight bravely against the Romans.* But Zadok was startled when Jesus' voice suddenly became gentle.

"Five sparrows are sold in the marketplace for a couple of pennies," He said. "And yet each one of those sparrows is important to God. Think of all the flocks of sparrows in the world—and I tell you, God never forgets about even one of them. God cares about the small things, the things that seem unimportant. He goes so far as to count each and every hair on your head. So don't be afraid. You are worth much more to God than all the flocks of sparrows!"

The love and joy in Jesus' voice made Zadok suddenly wish he were a little child again. For some strange reason, he longed to turn his head against his father's shoulder and cry. "Foolish," he muttered to himself. "Don't be silly."

Jesus was still talking, but Zadok missed what He was saying. Now a man in the crowd interrupted Him, shouting out, "Teacher, tell my brother he has to share with me the property our father left us."

Jesus turned to look at the man. "What gives Me the right to divide the property between you and your brother?" He asked. Then He turned back to the crowd. "Be careful about being greedy. Money is not important in My kingdom. Your true life has nothing to do with how many things you own."

How could money not be important? Zadok wondered. Could Jesus get soldiers and weapons without money? Money was one of the reasons why Zadok wanted to get rid of the Romans so badly; without the Roman taxes, his family would have enough money for a larger home, for fine clothes for them all, for gold dishes and soft rugs. . . When the Romans were gone, a load of fish like he and his father had caught today would bring them enough profit that they could be nearly rich.

His father nudged him with his elbow, interrupting his thoughts. "Listen," Simon whispered. "He's telling one of His stories."

Zadok turned his attention back to Jesus.

"Once there was a wealthy man who owned a huge piece of rich, fertile land," Jesus said. "Every year the land bore so many good crops, that each year's harvest was bigger than the last. At last the man began to think to himself, *I have more crops than I can store. What am I going to do with such a large harvest?*

"The man lay awake at night, thinking about all he could do with the money he would get from his crops. This year's harvest had been so great he knew he would be wealthier than he had ever been before. 'What should I do with all my money?' he asked himself happily.

" 'I know,' he said to himself. 'I will tear down all my barns and build even bigger ones. Then I will have plenty of room to store my grain. I will build a huge complex of buildings, so that I will have a place to keep all the things I am going to buy this year. And when everything is built, I will sit back and smile. "Lucky man!" I will tell myself. "You have everything you need. Take life easy! Eat, drink, and enjoy yourself!" '

"The man laughed out loud as he thought these things.

He rolled over on his back, his hands behind his head, and stared up at the dark ceiling, smiling to himself.

" 'Fool!'

"The soft voice made the man jump with terror. He sprang up in his bed, staring around the dark room. 'Who's there?'

"But there was no one there, no one but God.

" 'You fool,' the voice said sadly. 'This very night is the end of your life. Who will get all your money now? What good is it going to do you?' "

The crowd was very quiet as Jesus finished talking. He lowered His voice and added softly, "This is how it is with people who pile up riches for themselves and refuse to share with others. These people are rich in their own eyes—but they are poor in God's. And meanwhile, people who look poor to your eyes may truly be rich in God's kingdom."

The people began to murmur to each other, discussing the story they had just heard. Jesus turned to His disciples who were sitting closest to Him. "I'm telling you, you don't need to worry about things like food and clothes. Life is much more important than food, and your bodies are far more important than fine clothes. Look at the crows—God feeds them, doesn't He? And you are worth far more than birds! No matter how much you worry about something, your worrying doesn't do a bit of good. So why worry about anything? Your Father knows what you need."

Jesus looked down into Zadok's eyes. "God knows each and every one of you. He will give you what you need. You work for the kingdom, and God will take care of you."

Zadok took in a deep breath, filled with relief. There— Jesus was talking about setting up His kingdom, after all. Of course it made sense, he realized; if people were only worried about getting rich, they would never be able to work together to overthrow the Romans. Zadok thought of the Zealots who lived out in the hills, hard men who were willing to go without the comforts found in village life; these men were not tied down by the demands of a home and a family, and so they were more free to fight for their goal. Maybe Jesus wasn't so different from them. Zadok gave a Jesus a grin, longing to assure Him that he, Zadok, would never put riches ahead of the kingdom.

Jesus returned his gaze gravely, and suddenly Zadok squirmed uncomfortably, no longer so certain he knew what Jesus' story meant.

"Will your son be with us again tomorrow?" Jesus asked Simon.

Simon glanced at Zadok. Zadok didn't know if he wanted to hear Jesus again; something about the man made him uncomfortable. But his father nodded his head. "Yes. We will both be here."

Zadok did not go fishing with his father the next day. Instead, after their morning meal, he helped his mother grind enough wheat to last them a week. He hated the job, and as he blew the coarse flour out of his face, he wished they had enough money to hire a servant to help his mother. If they didn't have to pay so many taxes, none of them would have to work so hard. . . .

When his father came home at noon, they ate their lunch, and then he and Zadok went once more to the house where Jesus was staying. They walked with Jesus and the other disciples up into the hills, a growing crowd trailing behind them. As they walked, Jesus turned to Zadok.

"You have a such sad face today, Zadok. What are you thinking?"

Zadok hesitated, embarrassed, and then he burst out, "I am tired of the way things never change. The Romans grow more and more powerful, and we grow weaker and poorer. Doesn't God care about His people? Why doesn't He do something?"

Jesus looked thoughtful. "Do you ask God to help you?"

Zadok kicked a pebble out of his path. "Why should I?" he grumbled under his breath. "God doesn't hear His people's prayers anymore. He only listens to those who have power."

He had heard his father say the same words more than once, but now his father frowned at him and shook his head.

Zadok lifted his head defiantly. *Well, it's true,* he thought. He glanced up at Jesus' face, daring Him to contradict his thoughts. But Jesus only gave a small smile and began to tell another story.

"In a certain town," Jesus said, "—it doesn't really matter what town—there once was a judge who had no respect for anyone, not God and certainly not for other people. He was a hard, cold man, who totally lacked compassion.

"In the same town, there also lived a poor widowed woman who was having a legal problem. She had only a very little property to call her own, and someone was trying to take even that from her. She had no relatives to help her, and so she had no choice but to go to the judge and ask him for his help.

"But the judge was impatient with her little problem, and he barely listened to her complaints. The woman did not become discouraged, though. Day after day, she went back to the judge, and day after day she said, 'Please, Your Honor, help me. Take my side in this situation. I need your help.'

"The judge would wave his hand impatiently. 'Go away. I don't have time for you. I don't even care about your problem. Go away.'

"But the next day, the woman would be back again. 'Please, Your Honor, I need your help. Take my side in this situation.'

"At last the judge threw up his hands in exasperation. 'All right, all right,' he said. 'I couldn't care less what God thinks, and I couldn't care less what anyone else thinks about me. But I am sick of hearing this woman's voice every day. I will take her side. Otherwise, she will just keep coming, and she'll wear me out.' "

Jesus laughed as He finished His story. "So, Zadok, if this selfish judge finally listened to the widow, don't you think God will listen to you if you keep on asking Him for help?"

Zadok stuffed his hands in his pockets, trying to understand what Jesus meant. He glanced from the humor on Jesus' face to the puzzlement on his father's. "Do you mean," he asked slowly, "that God will answer our prayers because He gets impatient hearing us ask for the same thing over and over?"

Jesus was still smiling, as though He had told a joke. "No," He said, "God is not like the selfish judge. God loves His people. But the point is this: If even that bad judge eventually answered the woman's pleas, don't you think a God who loves His people will take action for them?"

"I don't know," Zadok answered honestly.

"The question is, Zadok, do God's people really seek His help? Or do they try to do it all on their own?" Jesus met Zadok's eyes for a moment longer, and then He added gently,

"Whose kingdom are you seeking, Zadok? God's? Or your own?"

Zadok opened his mouth—and to his surprise, he found he could not answer the question. His eyes dropped to his dusty toes, and he followed Jesus silently up the hillside.

When they reached the top of the hill, Jesus sat down and began to talk to the people. Zadok listened absently, his mind still on the story Jesus had told him. He barely noticed when a group of religious leaders pushed to the front of the crowd and began to ask Jesus questions, but he looked up when his father poked him.

"Listen to those men," Simon said under his breath. "They make me sick. They think they're so much better than the rest of us. You can tell from the way they stand there that they look down on us ordinary folk."

Zadok looked at the group of men in their rich robes. They held their heads high, and something about the tilt of their noses reminded Zadok of a group of caravan camels he had seen in the marketplace. He smothered a giggle and turned to see how Jesus would treat these men. Would He be impressed by their power?

But Jesus seemed to barely hear what the men were saying. Instead, He began to tell another story.

"Once there were two men who went up to the temple to pray. One of these men was a Pharisee, a very important religious leader who was powerful and well-respected. The other man collected taxes for the Romans, and everyone hated him.

"The Pharisee glanced at the tax collector, and his nostrils flared with distaste. Holding his robes close to him so they would not even brush against the other man, he moved past him, away from the other people who had also come to the temple. Everyone's eyes followed the Pharisee, and people murmured their respect, but he seemed to ignore them all. Instead, he turned his face upward and began to pray out loud.

" 'I thank You, God,' he said in a clear, carrying voice, 'that I am not greedy, like so many of the people here. Thank You that I'm not a liar, like some people I could mention, and thank You that I have kept my promises to my wife. And most of all, God, I really, truly thank You that I am not like that tax collector standing over there. What a poor excuse for a man! I, on the other hand, as You well know, go without eating two days a week, so that I can spend more time in prayer. And besides all that, I always give You one-tenth of all my money.' The Pharisee's face was filled with pride as he finished his prayer.

"Meanwhile, the tax collector stood at the back of the room, too ashamed to even lift his face toward heaven. He was so sorry for all the bad things he had done that he beat his fist against his chest. 'God, have pity on me!' he whispered. 'I am such a sinner.' "

Zadok could see that the religious leaders at the front of the crowd were clearly displeased with Jesus' story. But Jesus only smiled at them blandly. "When the two men went home from the temple," He said, "the tax collector was closer to God than the Pharisee. God was pleased with the tax collector's attitude—but He was not happy with the Pharisee's."

One of religious leaders reared his head back, and Zadok snickered, thinking again of a camel. "Do you mean to say," the man asked Jesus, "that God does not want us to pray and fast and tithe? That He doesn't care if we do all the things our religion asks us to do?"

"I'm saying," Jesus said quietly, "that if you think you are better than everyone else, you will eventually be put down. But if you humble yourself, you will find honor in God's kingdom."

People in the crowd began to shout out questions to Jesus, but He turned and wandered away through the people, stopping now and then to touch someone's shoulder, to smile and ask a question, to bend his head toward an old woman and listen to what she had to say. Zadok sat where he was, his chin in his hands, wondering what sort of kingdom Jesus was planning to build.

He glanced up at his father, who was sitting quietly

beside him. Simon hated tax collectors, he knew; his father had always called them selfish cowards who cared more for their own comfort than they did their own people, traitors who worked for the Romans and got rich from others' misfortunes. His father had no patience with the religious leaders either—but why would Jesus want a tax collector, even a sorry tax collector, in His kingdom?

Zadok was filled with a sudden, urgent need to understand. He got to his feet and followed Jesus through the crowd. He found Him sitting on the grass at the foot of the hill, surrounded by a group of children. Jesus was laughing out loud as the children crawled over Him, hanging on His shoulders and tugging at His hair.

Peter hurried past Zadok, scolding the children's mothers. "Call your children away! Don't you see the way they are bothering the Master?"

Jesus looked up at Peter and shook His head. "No, don't keep the children away from Me. The kingdom of God belongs to people like these little ones. No one can be a part of My kingdom who does not have a child's heart."

Zadok stood as though he were frozen, staring at Jesus. What possible use would children be in setting up a kingdom? A child's heart could not plan battle strategies or fight to the death for freedom. In each one of the stories he had heard Jesus tell, Jesus pointed out a person who was weak or unimportant or humble—and then claimed that this person would be an important part of His kingdom. With a terrible, cold sinking feeling, Zadok suddenly knew for certain that Jesus would never free them from the Romans.

Jesus settled a little girl in His lap, and then He looked over her head at Zadok. "Did you want to ask Me something, Zadok?"

Zadok shook his head and turned away. He blinked tears from his eyes and pushed his way through the people. He wanted to find his father and go home. What was the point of listening to anything else Jesus had to say?

During the next few weeks, Simon spent more and more time with Jesus. He asked Zadok to come with him, and sometimes Lydia went, too, but Zadok had lost all interest in the teacher from Nazareth. Jesus was just one more religious leader, Zadok had decided. Jesus clearly had no interest in rescuing His people from Rome's power, and nothing He had to say was of any use to Zadok.

"But, Son," Lydia said to him one evening as they made their way home after listening to Jesus teach, "don't you see that the kingdom of which Jesus speaks is far greater than the one you imagine?" She looked at Zadok's stubborn face, and she sighed in frustration. "You're like a beggar who asked that someone give him one copper coin—and then is angry when instead he receives a whole shower of gold. Do you not see how silly you're being?"

Zadok scowled at his mother. "I'm not being silly," he muttered. "What good will this mysterious kingdom of God do us if we are still oppressed by the Romans?"

Lydia shook her head. "What good would freedom from Rome do us if we are still slaves to our own sinful hearts?"

Zadok looked at his father, hoping Simon would say something to support Zadok's position. But his father was silent, his face thoughtful, and Zadok stomped ahead of his parents, impatient with them both. He longed for the days before Simon had become a disciple of Jesus of Nazareth, back when the world had seemed a simple, black-and-white place. Then he had known that the Romans were the enemy, the evil that he would give his life to fight. Now, against his will, Jesus was filling his head with new ideas, ideas that were too hard for him to grasp. He sighed with exasperation. And what good did it all do anyway? If they were all humble and simple, like children; if they spent all their time sharing their food with poor people and sick people; if they prayed all the time and said they were sorry for every bad thing they ever did—well, then the Romans would just get stronger and stronger, and the Jewish nation would be too busy being loving and humble to stop them. None of it made any sense to Zadok.

The next day, his parents brought him to hear Jesus again, and Zadok found he couldn't help but sympathize with the religious leaders who were grumbling about Jesus. Jesus was surrounded by a crowd of people who looked like outcasts to Zadok, tax collectors and cripples, ragged women and blind children. Zadok shook his head at the ragtag group and wondered why he had ever thought that Jesus would be able to lead them to freedom. He found himself nodding in agreement when he overheard a Pharisee say, "Look at this man! He welcomes the worst kind of people. He even sits down and eats with them!"

Zadok had started to turn away when he heard his father's voice ask Jesus a question. "Who is the greatest in the kingdom of heaven?"

Simon had been so quiet lately that Zadok was startled he would speak up like this. *Maybe he, too, is starting to question Jesus,* Zadok thought to himself hopefully. He pushed closer to Jesus to hear His answer.

Jesus reached out for one of the dirty children who were playing close to Him and lifted the child in His arms. "See this child? The greatest in the kingdom of heaven is the person who becomes like this little child. And whoever reaches out to a child like this, in reality reaches out to Me." He put the child down on the ground again and kissed the small head, then turned back to Simon. "Never look down on someone who is little and weak. These are the very people I came to bring into My kingdom." He glanced over at the group of religious leaders who had been listening scornfully. "I didn't come for the people who are satisfied with what they have already. I came to find the lost." Jesus turned and looked directly at Zadok, and a small smile flickered at the corners of His mouth. "Let me tell you some stories. Maybe then you will understand."

"Suppose you were a shepherd," Jesus said, "who spent your

time out in the hills watching over your sheep. You have a hundred sheep to care for, but one day one of them wanders away and gets lost in the rocks. What do you do? Do you say to yourself, 'Oh, well, I have ninety-nine sheep left—what does one little lost sheep really matter?' No, you make sure those ninety-nine are safe in the pasture, and then you go out to look for the one sheep that is lost. You search up and down the mountainsides, late into the night—and when at last you find that one poor sheep, you shout out loud with joy.

"Gently, you lift the sheep up onto your shoulders and carry it back home. When morning comes, you call all your friends and neighbors together and tell them, 'Guess what? I found my lost sheep! I'm so excited to have it back. Let's have a party to celebrate.' "

Jesus looked from face to face in the crowd that surrounded Him. "In the same way," He said, speaking slowly and clearly, "I tell you this: Heaven is happier about that one person who is lost and turns to God than it is about the ninety-nine who have no need to repent."

Zadok let out a long sigh of impatience. Now Jesus was talking about sheep and heaven, all in one breath, as though heaven were an actual place that Jesus knew well. *He must be crazy after all,* Zadok thought with disgust.

Jesus met Zadok's gaze. "Zadok," He said softly, "I promise you that if you turn back to God, heaven will celebrate. God longs to have you back. He doesn't want you to be lost anymore."

Zadok gulped, suddenly shaken. *But I haven't turned away from God,* he wanted to protest. *I'm not lost.* But then he remembered the long-ago days when he was small, when he had loved to pray with his parents before each meal and at the end of the day, when God had seemed real and wonderful to him—back before he had begun to hate the Romans. He opened his mouth, not sure what he wanted to say, but before he could think of anything, Jesus began to tell another story.

"Once there was a woman who had ten silver coins," Jesus said. "She was a thrifty woman, who ran her household carefully, and she was saving her money for something wonderful. But one day, she discovered that somehow she has lost one of those silver coins.

"So what do you think she does? Does she say to herself, 'Oh, well, it's only one coin. It's all right. After all, I have nine more.' No, each one of those coins was hard-earned, and each is precious to her. And so when she realizes that she has lost one, she lights a lamp and gets down on her knees and searches every nook and cranny of her house.

"And when, at last, she finds the lost coin, she sings with joy. She gets up and brushes off her robe, and then she runs out to tell all her friends. 'I'm so happy!' she cries. 'Come over to my house and celebrate with me.' "

Jesus fell silent. Then He added softly, "I tell you, Zadok, the angels of God rejoice in the same way when a sinner comes back to God."

Somehow, Zadok could not make himself look into Jesus' face. He hung his head, thinking, *First it's sheep and heaven, and now it's housewives and angels. He's crazy. He doesn't make any sense. None of this is important.* But somehow his heart told him that Jesus' words were important. He had a dizzy, uncomfortable feeling, as though everything he had believed for so long was crumbling around him. He raised his head and searched the crowd for his mother's face. When he found it, she was already looking at him, her eyes filled with such love that he blinked and looked away, embarrassed.

"I have one more story, Zadok," Jesus said, and then He raised His voice so that everyone could hear.

"There was once a man who had two sons. The older one was hardworking and responsible, but the younger one was only interested in enjoying himself and having a good time.

"One day, the younger son came to his father and said, 'Father, I don't want to wait until you die for my share of your property. Give it to me now.'

"So the father, who loved his sons very much, divided his property between the two young men.

"Only a few days later, the younger son took his share of the property and sold it. His father's heart broke as he watched his son pack his bags and leave home, but he did nothing to stop the young man.

"The younger son went down the road whistling, glad to leave behind the life he had lived in his father's house. He traveled to a distant country, and there he had a good time, spending his money on anything and everything. Before long, he had spent every cent of the sizable fortune his father had given him.

"At about the same time, a terrible famine hit the country where he was staying. There was not enough food to go around, even for those who had money, and the younger son had nothing. Desperate, he got a job with a farmer, who sent him to take care of his pigs.

"The young man's stomach was growling, and he was dizzy with hunger, but no one offered him anything to eat; apparently, he was expected to earn his food first. He was so desperate for food that he started to cram the pig food into his mouth, but one of the other workers saw him. 'Hey, you!' the other worker shouted. 'Stop that. The farmer won't like it if he hears you've been eating the food meant to fatten his pigs.'

"At that moment, the young man came to his senses. *My*

father's workers all have as much food as they want, he thought to himself, *and here I am starving to death. I might as well go back home.* As he shoveled out the pigsty, he planned the speech he would say to his father when he got home. 'Father,' he would say, 'I have sinned against God and against you. I'm no longer fit to be called your son, so please, treat me now like one of your hired workers.'

"He threw down his shovel and left the pig farm, suddenly so eager to be home that he could wait no longer.

"When he was still a long way down the road from his father's house, he saw someone running toward him. It was his father, running like a strong, young man, his robe blowing out behind him, his arms outstretched. 'Son,' he called. 'Son!' He reached the young man and threw his arms around him and kissed him.

"The young man immediately launched into his planned speech. 'Father, I have sinned against God and against you. I'm no longer fit to be called your son, so—'

"But before he could get any further, his father interrupted him by calling over his shoulder to his servants. 'Quick!' his father shouted. 'Go get some good clothes to put on my son. Get my gold ring out and put it on his finger. Put some shoes on his feet. And then go kill that calf we've been fattening up for a special occasion. We're going to have a party!' He turned back to his son with tears in his eyes, and his voice was tender now. 'For this son of mine was dead, but now he is alive. He was lost, but now I have found him again.'

"He gave his son another hug, and then the party began.

"But meanwhile the older son had been working hard for his father during all the time the younger son was away. Now, as he came in from working in the field, he could hear the music and dancing from inside the house. 'What's going on?' he called to one of the servants.

" 'Your brother has come back,' the servant answered. 'Your father is so happy to have him home safe and sound, he's thrown a big party. He even killed that prize calf of his he's been saving.'

"When the older son heard this, he was filled with anger and jealousy. He was so upset that he refused to even go inside the house.

"But his father came out to him. 'Please, Son, come inside and celebrate with us. Your brother is home!'

"The older brother bit his lip to keep back his rage. When he had himself under control, he said between his teeth, 'Look, all these years I have worked for you without ever complaining. I work as hard as any of your hired workers, and I have never once disobeyed you. And what have you given me? Nothing. You've never suggested that I throw even a little party for my friends. But when my little brother runs off with his inheritance and then comes back with nothing, what do you do? You kill your prize calf and throw an enormous party. You always did like him best. It's not fair.'

"His father couldn't help but laugh, even as he reached out and put his arm around his older son. 'Don't be silly, Son,' he said. 'You have your inheritance, just as your brother did. You and I are always together, and being with you makes me happy every day. Everything I have is yours. But today we are celebrating because your brother who was lost is found at last. I thought he was dead, but instead he is home and safe. Be happy with us, Son. You know how much I love you.' "

Zadok and his parents were quiet as they walked home that evening. As they reached their house, Lydia said softly, "What do you think the older brother did?"

"What do you mean?" Zadok asked her as he followed her inside.

"When his father told him how much he loved him and asked him to celebrate with him." She began to get out the food for their supper. "Do you think the older brother joined the party? Or do you think he still refused to come inside?"

Simon lit the fire. "I hope he had enough sense to come inside with his father. Anger and hatred are poor companions, I've learned. They eat you up inside and leave you with nothing."

Lydia smiled up at her husband, then reached to press a

kiss against his cheek. "You've changed, Simon," she said.

He looked back at her. "I suppose I have." He glanced at his son and added, "I thought I had to change the world by overthrowing the Roman government. But Jesus has taught me that the most important change has to happen inside my own heart."

Zadok looked back and forth between his parents. The quiet joy he saw in their faces filled him with rage. What good would all this love and gentleness do anyone? It would not put food on their table or pay their taxes. It would leave the smug Romans in power, and the Jews would be as poor as ever.

He wanted to shout at them and make them see how wrong they were. But it wasn't their fault, he realized; it was Jesus of Nazareth who had confused them.

Zadok pressed his lips tight together. The next time he saw Jesus, Zadok was going to speak his mind.

CHAPTER 6

Zadok had his chance the next week when his parents again went to sit at Jesus' feet and listen to Him teach. As soon as they were settled, Jesus leaned forward and looked into Zadok's eyes, as if He knew Zadok had something he wanted to say. "Well, Zadok?"

Zadok felt his face turn red, but he raised his chin and said, "My father followed You at first because he thought You were the One we were waiting for, the Messiah, the One who would lead us to freedom. But he was wrong." His mother kicked him in the back with her sandal, but he ignored her and held his ground, his head high. "Just what sort of kingdom do You think all Your talk will lead to?"

Jesus looked into Zadok's face calmly. "An eternal kingdom, Zadok. A kingdom that lasts forever. A kingdom where you will never die."

His answer took Zadok by surprise. Zadok gulped and fell silent. He tried to think of a response, something that would get the conversation back on track, but before he could say anything, a teacher of Jewish Law stepped forward and asked, "Teacher, what act must I perform to live forever?"

Jesus turned toward the man. "Well, what do the Scriptures say? How do you interpret them?"

The man answered immediately, "The Scriptures say to love the Lord your God with all your heart, with all your soul, with all your strength, and with all your mind." He obviously knew this answer by heart. "And," he added, "love your neighbor as yourself."

"That's right," Jesus replied. "Keep on doing this and you will live forever."

The teacher of the Law shifted his weight from foot to foot. "Well, then," he asked uncomfortably, "who is my neighbor?"

Jesus smiled. "That's a good question. Let Me tell you a story."

"There was once a man," Jesus said, "who was traveling the dangerous road between Jerusalem and Jericho. As happens to so many travelers along that road, he was attacked by robbers who beat him up, took everything he had, and then left him half-dead beside the road.

"A priest came along the road. He saw the injured man lying there all bloody, but he knew he would get himself dirty if he touched the man. 'Surely,' he said to himself, 'God doesn't want me to touch this man. He could be someone who isn't a Jew, or he could be dead. If I touched him, I would be breaking the Law. I have just come from serving God in the temple, and it would be bad for my spiritual condition if I lowered myself by getting mixed up with this terrible situation.'

"And so the priest crossed to the other side of the road and hurried on by.

"Next, one of the temple helpers came along the road. He stopped for a moment and looked at the wounded man, but the man looked so terrible lying there covered with blood that the temple helper could not bring himself to touch him. He, too, hurried across the road and went on his way, leaving the man alone and in agony.

"But before long a man from Samaria came down the road. Of course, the Jews hate Samaritans and think they are all violent and dangerous, but when this Samaritan saw the wounded man, his heart was filled with pity. He immediately went to him and bent down to help him. He put medicine and bandages on his wounds, and then he lifted him onto his donkey. The Samaritan took the wounded man to an inn, and there he cared for him until the man was well enough for the Samaritan to leave him. Before the Samaritan left, he gave enough money to the innkeeper to provide for the man until he was totally recovered."

Jesus looked at the teacher of the Law. "Which of these three men would you say was a neighbor to the wounded man?"

The teacher looked down at the ground. "The one who showed real love," he said in a low voice.

"Exactly," Jesus agreed. "Now if you want to live forever, you go and do the same."

The teacher stood still for a moment, looking as though he wanted to say something and yet could not quite bring himself to speak the words out loud. At last, with a sigh, he walked away. Jesus looked after him for a moment, and then He turned back to Zadok. "Do you want to live forever, Zadok?"

Zadok shrugged, though his heart was beating hard. "No one lives forever."

Jesus shook His head. "In My kingdom, Zadok, no one dies." He smiled. "You have had your eyes fixed on an earthly kingdom, one where the Jews would be free of Roman power. But all along, I have been talking about a heavenly kingdom, one that is far greater than anything you could ever imagine. Which kingdom do you choose, Zadok?"

For some reason, Zadok felt his eyes burn. He stared straight ahead. "When will this kingdom of Yours come, then?" he asked, his voice hard and flat.

Jesus shook His head again. "No, Zadok, you're still thinking of another sort of kingdom. My kingdom is not made of something you can see and touch. You won't be able to say, 'Here it is!' or 'Look, it's over there!' The kingdom of God is here, Zadok." Jesus stretched out His hand and touched first Zadok's heart and then his forehead. "It is within you."

"I don't understand," Zadok whispered. He blinked away the tears that threatened to spill out of his eyes.

"It's not so complicated, really," Jesus said gently. "Think about the story I just told you. How can your heart lead you to the kingdom of heaven?"

Zadok looked into Jesus' dark eyes, and he saw the love there. He felt his mother close beside him, and then his father's hand dropped on his shoulder. He knew he was surrounded by love. Was this the kingdom that Jesus talked about?

But he had hated the Romans so long. How could he allow Jesus to take that hatred out of his heart? What would there be to take its place? All he had wanted was freedom for their nation. Who would he be if he allowed something else to be more important to him? He looked up doubtfully from his mother to his father, trying to see the answer in their faces.

"It's simple," his mother said. "Love is what draws you to the kingdom of heaven."

His father's hand squeezed his shoulder tight. "I'm sorry, Son, that I confused you with my own anger against the Romans. I still want freedom for our nation. But your mother is right. Love is the most important thing—like the teacher of the Law just said. If you love God with all your heart and soul and mind, you will give yourself to Him. And if you love your neighbor, then you treat everyone you meet with the same concern you would want them to show you. Doing that is more important than how much money we have or what kind of clothes we wear." Simon looked at Jesus. "If I understand right, love is the door that leads us into the Master's kingdom—and His kingdom will last forever. Not even death can end it."

Zadok turned from his parents to Jesus. He thought of all of Jesus' stories, and suddenly they all began to make sense. Jesus nodded. "Come back to Me, Zadok. Give your heart away. Be a part of My kingdom. Will you?"

For a moment, Zadok was too scared to say anything. But then he looked into Jesus' eyes, and his fear disappeared. He took a deep breath. "Yes," he said, and he saw Jesus' face fill with joy.

THE TWELVE DISCIPLES

by Ellyn Sanna

CHAPTER 1

While she waited for her mother, twelve-year-old Tamar curled her bare toes in the cool dust beneath her great-grandmother's fig tree. From inside the house, she could hear the high, fast murmur of her mother's voice. Her mother was upset with her, because Tamar had refused to go to the First Day service yesterday. Now her mother had brought Tamar to Grandma Mary's home so that the two women could discuss what should be done with a girl who refused to gather with the other Christians.

Tamar suspected that her great-grandmother was even angrier with her than her mother was. After all, Grandma Mary spent nearly her entire life talking in prayer to the Master. No matter how dangerous it was for Christians to gather together, no matter how much her old bones ached, Grandma Mary never missed a single First Day service. Tamar sighed, imagining the sorrow in her great-grandmother's eyes when she heard that the youngest member of her family was still refusing to worship the Lord.

"You're a coward," Tamar's older brother Daniel had accused yesterday when he found Tamar hiding in the alley behind their house. "You're too scared to share the Lord's meal." His lip had curled with scorn; remembering, Tamar blinked away tears. Daniel was only two years older than she was, but because their father was dead, Daniel was the man of the family. He always acted as though he was at least thirty, as though he was far more wise and mature than Tamar, as though he was never doubtful or worried or frightened. . . . Tamar rested her forehead on her knees and screwed her eyes shut. "I'm not a coward," Tamar whispered. "I'm not."

"No," agreed a soft, quavery voice. "I have never thought of you as a coward. After all, you are the one who has always liked to play with snakes and beetles."

Tamar looked up into her great-grandmother's wrinkled face. "Snakes and beetles are different," she muttered.

Her great-grandmother smiled. "Oh, yes. I' would say so. They're ugly things that bite and sting. But my Master is altogether lovely, and He gives us only love and joy."

Tamar sighed. Grandma Mary always insisted on talking about Jesus as though He had just stepped out of the courtyard, when instead He had been dead for almost seventy years.

Her grandmother put her hand on Tamar's head. "Come, Child. Help me climb up on the roof. I would like to talk with you where we won't be disturbed."

Reluctantly, Tamar scrambled to her feet. She didn't want Grandma Mary to be sad or upset; but she also hated to go up on the roof with her grandmother where anyone in the street below might look up and see them. Everyone in the village knew Grandma Mary was a Christian. And being a Christian was against the law. The last thing Tamar wanted was to be arrested and hauled off to Rome.

Grandma Mary climbed up the steep steps to the roof so slowly that Tamar had to bite her lip to hold in her impatience. She gripped her grandmother's elbow firmly, hoping the old woman would not stumble and fall. At last, they reached the rooftop, and with a tiny moan, Grandma Mary settled herself on the flat clay surface. She smoothed the folds of her mantle over her legs, then leaned back against the roof's railing and smiled.

"Your mother tells me you no longer wish to take the Lord's meal with the rest of us on First Days."

Tamar looked down at her hands. "That's right," she mumbled.

"Hmm." Grandma Mary pursed her lips thoughtfully. "Many of our brothers and sisters are afraid to gather together these days. They live in fear of Emperor Trajan's law against Christians. But I know you are not a coward."

Tamar felt Grandma Mary studying her face, but she refused to meet her grandmother's eyes. After a long, silent moment, the old woman asked gently, "Why are you so upset, Child?"

Tamar hesitated. "Because of Flavia," she said finally. "Flavia was my friend. And someone wrote a letter to the governor, accusing Flavia and her family of being Christians. The soldiers came and took them away, all of them, even Flavia's little brother." Tamar blinked away the tears that flooded her eyes. "I heard last week that the emperor had them put to death," she finished in a whisper.

Without a word, Grandma Mary put out her arms and pulled Tamar close. Tamar felt her grandmother trembling, and when at last she moved away from Grandma Mary, she saw the tears that streaked the old woman's cheeks. "We have lost so many," Grandma Mary said softly. "So many of the Lord's followers have been wiped out."

Tamar scrubbed her wet face with her fists. "Then what's the point, Grandma? In the end, we'll all be killed. No one will be left who even remembers your Master's name. Shouldn't we just live as quietly as possible, so that no one will notice us? At least that way, there'd be a chance someone would live to hand down the stories to their children. Don't you think that would make sense to God? Don't you think He'd understand if we just stayed home on First Day from now on?"

Grandma Mary smiled. For a long, silent moment, she simply looked up at the blue sky above their heads. The railing began to poke into Tamar's back, and she shifted back and forth uneasily; she never knew what to do when she knew her grandmother was talking to Jesus inside her head.

When Grandma Mary finally looked back at her great-granddaughter, Tamar burst out, "I don't want to be killed. And I don't want you or Mother or Daniel to be killed, either."

Grandma Mary reached up a small, gnarled hand and smoothed a strand of hair away from Tamar's hot face. "The Lord loved us enough to give His life," she said softly. "If we love Him, we will be willing to do the same. Look at Jesus' disciples, Child, His closest friends. Many of them have died for their faith." She smiled. "I am ready to follow their example."

Tamar's fingers curled into fists. "Well, I'm not!" She bit her lip to stop the other fierce, angry words that threatened to spill out of her mouth. After a moment, she sucked in a deep breath and said more quietly, "I'm not like the disciples, Grandma Mary. They knew Jesus, the way you know Him. But I don't. I don't know. . ." She wasn't sure if she should go on, but after a moment, in a voice barely louder than a whisper, she finished, "I'm don't know if He's worth dying for." She stared defiantly at her grandmother. "And the more Mother and Daniel argue with me, the less convinced I feel."

To her surprise, Grandma Mary laughed.

"What's so funny?" Tamar asked suspiciously.

Her grandmother shook her head. "I was just remembering Philip, one of the Lord's twelve disciples. I think he would have understood your predicament, Child."

Tamar had grown up hearing stories about the disciples, for her great-grandmother had also followed Jesus of Nazareth. As a young woman, Grandma Mary had been known as Mary Magdalene, and she had been close friends with Jesus and His group of twelve men.

But Tamar didn't want to hear about Philip now, and she didn't want to hear one of her grandmother's stories about Jesus. When Grandma Mary said nothing more, though, Tamar began to feel curious in spite of herself. "Why?" she asked finally. "What happened to Philip?"

Her grandmother gave her a small, pleased smile. Tamar sighed and settled herself more comfortably against the roof's railing.

"Like so many of the disciples," Grandma Mary began, "Philip was a fisherman from Bethsaida, a little town on the Sea of Galilee. He was the very first disciple Jesus chose.

" 'Come, be My disciple,' Jesus said to Philip.

"I suspect Philip had known Jesus and listened to Him talk for quite awhile before this. So Philip was excited and honored when Jesus asked him to be His disciple. But before Philip did anything else, he went to find his friend Nathanael. He wanted to share the good news. 'We have found the very person Moses and the prophets wrote about!' he told his friend. 'His name is Jesus, the son of Joseph from Nazareth.'

" 'Nazareth!' exclaimed Nathanael. 'Can anything good come from there?'

"Philip didn't bother to argue with him. 'Come and see for yourself,' was all he said, and he brought Nathanael to Jesus. You see, sometimes arguing with a person doesn't do any good. Sometimes it's better to simply show them the truth and let them make up their own minds.

"Later, Jesus did the same thing to Philip himself. It happened one time when Jesus was trying to spend some time alone with His disciples in the hills beside the Sea of Galilee. Jesus had just sat down at the top of a hill with His friends, when He looked up and saw a huge crowd coming toward them.

"He turned to Philip and asked, 'Where can we buy bread for all these people?'

"Philip looked down over the crowds' heads and mentally did a quick tally. He shook his head, for he could tell there must be five thousand men and their families coming toward them. 'It would take eight months' wages to feed this many people!'"

"Jesus didn't bother to argue with Philip. Instead, He simply proceeded to feed all those people, using one small lunch.

"Of course, Jesus could have tried to make His point by giving Philip a long lecture on God's bountiful care for each and every person. But instead of telling Philip, He showed him.

"By the time the disciples were in the Upper Room eating their last supper with the Lord, Philip had begun to get the picture. So when Jesus started talking about His Father, Philip said simply, 'Lord, show us the Father, and we will be satisfied.'

"But Jesus knew that Philip still didn't really understand Who He was. 'Philip,' He said, 'after all this time I've been with you, don't you understand yet what I've been showing you all along? I have shown you the Father already! If you've seen Me, then you've seen the Father. I am in the Father, and the Father is in Me.'

"Finally, all Philip's questions were answered. All he needed to do was look at Jesus."

Grandma Mary turned to look into Tamar's face. "I won't argue with you about First Day, Child. I know you have many fears and questions. So from now on, whenever you and I are together, I am going to tell you about the lives of Jesus' disciples. They were men who looked at Jesus and found the answers to all their fears and doubts. Maybe their lives will help show you the answer as well."

CHAPTER 2

The next morning, Tamar brought her great-grandmother a bucket of water from the village well. She had hoped to escape quickly, without another story from her grandmother, but Grandma Mary caught her sleeve and stopped her as she turned to go.

"Sit down a moment, Child. I have been thinking about you all night. Are you still determined to stay home when First Day comes again?"

Reluctantly, Tamar sank down on the wooden bench where her grandmother was sitting. "I don't want to gather with the other Christians anymore," she mumbled, her eyes on the water bucket beside her feet. She let out a long breath, then looked up at Grandma Mary. "I don't want you and Daniel and Mother to go, either. Daniel thinks he can handle whatever happens, but he's too young. He doesn't understand that it's too dangerous. He says I'm a coward—but I say you're all being foolish!"

Tamar looked down at the ground where drips of water had made little circles in the dust. She waited for Grandma Mary to rebuke her, but her grandmother was silent. After a long moment, Tamar could no longer bear the silence. "I'm not a coward," she said fiercely. "Being stupid is different than being brave. You wouldn't call me a coward if I refused to jump off the cliffs into the sea. But right now, meeting with the other Christians is just as foolhardy. Why should we risk danger when we don't have to?"

"Hmm," Grandma Mary said, "I don't think gathering together to celebrate the Lord's meal has much to do with whether we are brave or cowardly, foolish or wise. I think it has more to do with whether we love the Master."

"But meeting with the other Christians is against the law, Grandma Mary. If you want to believe in Jesus, why can't all of you do it secretly, inside your heads, where no one else can see? I'm sure Jesus would understand."

"You remind me of one of the Lord's closest friends, Tamar. Always so impulsive, so sure you're right, so quick to talk your way out of a corner. You're so much like Simon Peter."

Tamar rolled her eyes. She knew, of course, that Peter had been one of the church's greatest leaders; some even called him the father of the faith, for he had traveled around the world preaching and building churches. Tamar was pretty certain she didn't have much in common with Simon Peter, who had served his Lord so fearlessly. But when Grandma Mary was in a mood to tell a story, there was no stopping her.

"Simon Peter wasn't always the way he was when he was

older," Grandma Mary said. "No, when he was a young man, he was a lot like you, Tamar. He liked to talk and laugh; he was quick to get angry with his brother Andrew, just like you lose your temper with Daniel; and as much as Peter loved Jesus, he couldn't quite believe that the Lord could really keep him safe. But if anyone should have trusted Jesus, it was Peter. After all, he was one of the first of us to follow the Lord.

"When Simon was a man in his thirties, he was living with his wife and her family over in Capernaum. You know where that is, don't you, Tamar? It's over on the north shore of the Sea of Galilee, just west of the Jordan River. He and his younger brother Andrew were fishermen. Simon owned his own boat, and the two brothers were partners with old Zebedee, another boat owner.

"Simon and his family were very religious. They obeyed the Jewish Laws; they worshiped often in the synagogue; and they went to Jerusalem for all the holy days. Simon had a good life, and he wasn't looking to change anything about it. Still, he was always restless, and he loved to hear new ideas—just like you, Tamar. He also was sick of the Romans ruling our country, and he was hoping that God would send the Messiah, someone who would free our people.

"So Simon was pretty excited one day when his brother came running up to him, shouting, 'We have found the Messiah!' Immediately, Simon dropped the fishing nets he had been mending. He ran after Andrew, back to the place where Jesus was staying.

"Jesus took one look at Simon and said, 'You are Simon, son of John. From now on your name shall be Peter, the rock.' You see, right from the beginning, the Lord looked into Peter's heart and saw that underneath all those quick feelings that jumped from happy to angry to excited in less than a minute, underneath all that was something as solid and dependable as a rock. Jesus could always see a person's true nature. Or maybe He just saw what a person was meant to be.

"Anyway, Peter soon became the spokesman for Jesus' little band of followers. When they were confused or frightened, he was the one who had the courage to speak up and ask the Lord what was going on. And he was quick to put his faith in Jesus.

"After that first meeting with Jesus, Peter and Andrew went back to their fishing boats. But a few weeks later, one morning after they had been out fishing all night, Jesus came along and asked if He could come on board.

" 'Go out into deep water,' the Lord said. 'And then lower your nets for a catch.'

" 'Master,' Peter protested, 'we've been fishing all night, and we're exhausted. We didn't catch a single fish anyway. There's just nothing out there right now.'

"Well, Peter had been fishing those waters for nearly

twenty years, and he certainly knew his business. Jesus was the son of a carpenter, so by rights He shouldn't have known anything about fishing. But already Peter was beginning to understand that this was no ordinary man. Peter looked into Jesus' face, and then he shrugged. 'Whatever You say, Lord.' He turned to Andrew with a sigh. 'Let's go fishing.'

"So they took the boat out into deep water, and down went the nets—and almost instantly, they could feel the nets dragging on the boat with an enormous weight! They had caught such a huge school of fish that their nets began to split, and they had to get Zebedee and his sons to come help them.

"When they were all safely back on dry land, Peter threw himself at the Lord's feet. 'Leave me, Lord!' he cried. 'I am too far away from God to be in Your company.'

"You see, Peter knew right then that Jesus was someone different from anyone he had ever met before. He sensed that being with Jesus was going to demand everything Peter had, all his strength and courage and loyalty—and poor Peter wasn't sure he was strong enough for the challenge. He would rather have walked away from the Lord right then than risked failing.

"But like I said, Jesus knew the strength that was hidden inside Peter. In fact, Jesus knew Peter better than Peter knew himself, and Jesus knew what Peter would be able to do once he opened his heart to God. So Jesus just smiled. 'Don't be afraid,' He told Peter. 'You used to be a fisherman—but I will make you a fisher of men instead.'

"Peter put his fears out of his mind and followed Jesus. Pretty soon, though, he began to realize that Jesus was not a human hero, someone who was going to rescue His people from earthly dangers. Peter was the first of the disciples to put into words Who Jesus really was when some of Jesus' followers had tried to make Him King.

"People were pretty disappointed when Jesus refused to cooperate, and along about then, a lot of people gave up on Jesus and stopped following Him. So Jesus asked His closest friends if they, too, were going to desert Him.

" 'Where would we go, Lord?' Peter said. 'You are the only One Who has the words that show us the way to eternal life. We believe in You. We know that You are the Christ, the Son of the living God.'

"You could see that Jesus was pleased with what Peter had said. 'You are Peter, the rock,' He said. 'On the foundation stone of your faith, Peter, I will build My church.'

Peter couldn't help but puff up with pride at Jesus' words. He liked to be praised, just like we all do, and he also liked to be reassured that Jesus loved him as much as He did His other friends. But then while Peter was sitting there grinning from ear to ear, Jesus said something else that wiped the smile right off Peter's face.

" 'We'll be going to Jerusalem soon,' Jesus said, almost

like He was talking to Himself. 'I will suffer greatly there at the hands of the religious leaders. Eventually, they will kill Me. And then I will be raised on the third day.

"Peter looked at Jesus as though He had lost His mind. 'Don't talk like that, Master!' he cried. He figured that Jesus must be worrying about His safety, and so Peter tried to drive the fear out of His mind. 'I won't let anything happen to You, Lord,' Peter promised. 'And I certainly won't let anyone kill You.'

"The moment before Jesus had been praising Peter—but now He looked straight at Peter and said, 'Get out of My sight, you Satan! You are trying to make Me trip and fall. You are looking at things from a human perspective instead of God's.'

"Peter turned bright red. He didn't dare argue with the Lord, so he just turned away. But he couldn't get Jesus' words out of his head, and he worried about them all the while he and the other disciples traveled with Jesus. As he watched Jesus preaching and healing, though, he wondered if Jesus was doing the right thing. If Jesus were really in danger from the religious leaders, wouldn't He be smarter to live His life a little more quietly? Did He really have to make such a spectacle of Himself by working so many miracles? Did He have to draw everyone's attention by spending so much time with poor people and sick people and women?

"But a few days later, when Jesus had taken the disciples up onto Mount Tabor for some rest, something happened that made Peter forget all about his worries, at least for the time being. Jesus took His three closest friends, Peter, James, and John, high up into the mountain for some time alone—and while Jesus was spending time praying to His Father, Peter saw something that filled him with wonder and awe.

"Suddenly, Jesus began to shine! His clothes and His skin were so bright that they dazzled Peter's eyes. And then Peter saw that two other men were with Jesus—Moses and Elijah, heroes of the faith whom Peter knew had been dead for hundreds of years. They didn't look like ghosts, though, all wispy and see-through. Instead, all three men were lit up as though they were filled with some amazing life, a life that Peter had never even imagined. They looked more real and solid than anything Peter had seen before; compared to them, the rocks and trees around them looked like ghosts.

"After awhile, Elijah and Moses disappeared, and the strange, brilliant light faded from Jesus' skin and clothes. James and John were dumbfounded, silent with awe, but Peter blurted out, 'Master, what a wonderful experience! Let's build three shrines here, one for You, one for Moses, and one for Elijah.'

"It was one of those silly things people say before they think, the sort of thing that must have made Peter blush later whenever he thought of it. All he knew then, though, was that something wonderful had happened. He thought if he could put up some sort of permanent building for each shining figure, then he would be able to make this wonderful experience stay with him forever.

"Of course, faith doesn't work like that. We can't live in shrines built to yesterday's experiences; instead, we must simply walk day by day with the Lord, in shining moments and in dull ones. Luckily, before Peter could say any more silly things, a cloud settled over them, hiding the sun's light. From the midst of the cloud, they all heard a voice saying, 'This is My Son, My Beloved. Listen to Him!'

"A lot of Peter's fears disappeared after that day. In fact, now he had so much faith in Jesus that he dared do something that seemed truly foolhardy.

"One day, when the disciples were out on the Sea of Galilee in Peter's boat, a storm came up in the night. As morning came, they were still battling against the wind and rough water, when they saw a strange figure coming toward them through the waves.

" 'It's a ghost!' Peter cried out, and the other disciples began to scream with fear.

"But then a familiar voice calmed them. 'Get hold of yourselves, fellows! It's Me. Don't be afraid!'

"Peter leaned against the ship's railing, peering through the storm, trying to make out this person Who stepped so calmly on top of the water. 'Lord,' he shouted, 'if it's really You, then tell me to come to You across the water.'

"Jesus laughed and motioned to him with His hand. 'Come on, then!'

"And before Peter could think twice, he jumped out of the water and started striding off across the waves to meet the Master. That was Peter for you—filled with fear one minute, and brave as a lion the next.

"And then the next minute, he was scared all over again! Peter must have realized what he was doing—and it just didn't make any sense to him that he was walking on water. You see, he knew about faith, but he also knew about being sensible—and he hadn't figured out how to put the two together. As soon as he began thinking about what made sense, he began to sink.

"Of course, Jesus didn't let His friend drown. Smiling a sad smile, the Lord reached out and saved Peter.

"Even then, Peter still had a lot of lessons to learn. The night before our Lord's death, Jesus taught His friends about love and humility by washing their feet. When it was Peter's turn to have the dust and grime washed off his toes, though, he tucked his feet under his robe and shook his head. 'No! I will never let You wash my feet, Lord. It's just not right.'

"Again, Jesus shook His head sadly at His friend. 'But if I don't wash you, Peter, you won't belong to Me.'

"At that, Peter thrust out not only his feet but his hands

and his head, too. 'Then wash the rest of me, as well!' he cried. That was the way Peter was, you see. Whichever direction he jumped, he jumped with his whole weight. He always meant well, and he was no coward—but sometimes he let his fears push him in one direction instead of another.

"Later that evening, as Jesus continued to talk to His friends, Peter's fears got the best of him again. Jesus was talking as though He planned on leaving the disciples soon. Finally, Peter burst out, 'Lord, where are You going?'

"Jesus just smiled at him, and there was a hint of sadness in His face. 'You can't go with Me now, Peter, but you will follow Me later.'

" 'But why can't I come now, Lord?' Peter protested. 'I'm ready to die for You if I have to!'

"Jesus shook His head. 'Die for Me? No, Peter, you're not ready for that yet. In fact, before the rooster crows tomorrow morning, you will deny three times that you even know Me.'

"Later that night, Jesus and His friends went to a grove of olive trees that was one of Jesus' favorite places. While they were there, the soldiers came and arrested Jesus. Peter was determined to prove to Jesus that he would never deny Him, and so, without thinking, Peter grabbed a sword and cut off the ear of the high priest's servant.

" 'Put your sword away, Peter,' Jesus said. 'I'm ready to do My Father's will.'

"The soldiers took Jesus away, but Peter followed them. While the high priest questioned Jesus, Peter stood waiting in the courtyard, warming himself by the fire. One of the women servants noticed him and asked, 'Aren't you one of Jesus' disciples?'

"Peter was terrified. He didn't want to be arrested and dragged away by the soldiers. Before he could even think, the words spilled out of his mouth: 'No, I'm not.'

"Poor Peter. He huddled beside the fire, his face turned away from the others, feeling miserable and scared. *Surely, Jesus understands,* he told himself. After all, what good would it do Jesus if Peter was arrested, too?

"Another servant glanced sideways at Peter and then looked again. 'Aren't you one of Jesus' disciples?' he asked, just as the woman had earlier.

"And again Peter shook his head. 'No,' he said firmly. 'I never even met the man.'

"But one of the other men was staring at Peter's face. 'Didn't I see you out in the olive grove with Jesus?'

"This time Peter was so upset that he cursed. 'I swear to you, I don't know the man!'

"Just then, the rooster crowed, and Peter remembered what Jesus had said earlier that night. Peter turned away from the fire and left the courtyard, his face wet with tears.

"That could have been the end of Peter's story. Overcome with shame and guilt, he could have chosen to turn away from the Master forever. But Peter let his pride go. He went back to wait with the other disciples through that long, dark night, and the even longer, darker day that followed.

"And on the third day, when I went to Jesus' grave and found it empty, an angel gave me a message especially for Peter, even though Peter had denied the Lord. The angel told me to go and tell Peter that Jesus had risen from the dead. And when Jesus came to us with His new risen body, He forgave Peter. Jesus told Peter to be a shepherd to His people after Jesus had gone back to His Father.

"Peter did as Jesus had told him. He was still Peter, emotional and stubborn and impulsive. But after the Holy Spirit came to us, Peter was no longer swayed by his fears and his 'common sense.' Instead, he opened his heart wide to Jesus' Spirit. And Simon Peter became as dependable as the rock Jesus had always said he would be. He was a fearless preacher, one of our greatest leaders during our early days.

"So you see, sometimes we have to forget about our fears; we have to stop worrying about whether we're acting foolishly. Instead, we just have to look at Jesus. When we do, like Peter we'll be able to walk across all the stormy troubles that fill our lives. The wind of fear won't blow us back and forth anymore, because when our hearts are fixed on Jesus, our lives will be as solid as rock."

Grandma Mary turned and looked into Tamar's face. "Do you understand, Child?"

Tamar sighed. She knew what her grandmother was trying to say to her, but she couldn't let go of her worries. Not yet. It was different for Grandma Mary; like Peter, Grandma Mary had actually seen Jesus. She had touched Him and listened to His voice and smiled into His eyes. But Tamar had never seen Jesus, and sometimes it was hard for her to believe He was worth risking everything. She still had a hard knot of fear and sorrow in her stomach whenever she thought of Flavia and her family.

Tamar looked away from her grandmother's bright eyes. Why did Grandma Mary always look as though she knew some joyful secret? Tamar let out another long sigh and pleated her robe into tiny folds with her nervous fingers. "What happened to Peter?" she asked. "I mean, in the end? Was he safe?"

"Of course he was safe," Grandma Mary said serenely. "There is nothing that can separate us from the love of God."

Tamar looked at her grandmother suspiciously. "But in the end was he arrested for being Jesus' follower?"

Grandma Mary laughed. "Oh, yes, he was. He was thrown into prison to await his trial, and without a doubt he would have been put to death. But in the middle of the night, Peter found his cell ablaze with light, and the chains that bound him fell from his wrists. He looked around sleepily, sure he was dreaming, but an angel tapped him impatiently on the side. 'Wake up!' the angel said. 'Get dressed and put your sandals on. Now, follow me.'

"Peter was still convinced he was dreaming, but he did what he was told and followed the angel out of the prison. No one stopped them, and one after another the gates opened up before them. Finally, Peter found himself walking down the street by himself—and he realized at last that he had truly escaped.

"He went to the house where we were all gathered to pray for him. When he knocked on the door, a servant girl named Rhoda went to see who was there. She heard Peter's voice, and she was so excited that she forgot to open the door. Instead, she ran back to us, shouting, 'Peter is at the door!'

"We couldn't believe her. 'You're out your mind,' one man told Rhoda. And a woman decided that Peter must have been killed. 'That must be his spirit at the door,' she said with a shiver.

"Meanwhile, though, poor Peter was still patiently knocking on the door. Finally, we all went out to see who was there. And then we hugged him and shouted and made so much noise that he had to tell us to be quiet before the guards heard all the commotion and came back to get him."

Remembering, Grandma Mary laughed so hard that tears came to her eyes. She wiped them away, shaking her head in delight at the happy memory. "You see, Child, the Lord takes care of us."

"The Lord doesn't always take care of us," Tamar said softly, still thinking of Flavia. She heard voices in the street below, and she tucked her chin down against her chest, hoping that no one would recognize her. "Did He always take care of Peter?"

"Of course, Child. After Peter escaped from prison, he continued to preach the good news. He traveled around the world, and he was a shepherd to us all, just as Jesus had told him to be. I lost touch with him years ago, but I heard that his wife and he traveled all the way across the world to faraway lands like Gaul and Britain. Eventually, Peter and his wife came back and settled in Rome, where they continued to introduce people to Jesus. I have heard people who met him describe him as such a 'humble, meek man, gentle, tender, loving, and lovely.'

"While he was in Rome, he spent some time with young John Mark. Later, when Mark wrote his story of Jesus' life, he included many of Peter's memories—and you know that we still read Mark's story on First Days when we gather together.

"Peter knew that we lived in dangerous times. After all, the emperor in those days was the evil Nero, who was even worse than Trajan. So he wrote letters of comfort and courage to the churches. He told us, 'Dear friends, don't be surprised at the fiery trials you are going through, as if something strange were happening to you. Instead, be very glad—because these trials will make you partners with Christ in His suffering, and afterward you will have the wonderful joy of sharing His glory when it is displayed to all the world.' "

Grandma Mary smiled at Tamar. "You see, Child, Peter wasn't afraid anymore. He still faced dangers in this world. But long ago, he had caught a glimpse of a world that was far more real than the one where we live. He knew that the pains and sorrows we face here will not last forever—but the joy that Jesus gives us will endure for eternity."

But Tamar remained unconvinced. "How did Peter die?" she insisted. "Did the Romans get him in the end?"

Her grandmother shrugged. "I heard from a friend that the Christians in Rome were as worried as you are now. They were afraid that Christianity would simply disappear and die if anything were to happen to Peter. So they persuaded Peter and his wife to leave Rome and go into hiding.

"But while Peter was sneaking away from Rome, I heard he had a vision of the Lord. In the vision, he saw Jesus walking in the opposite direction with a cross on His back.

" 'Lord, where are You going?' Peter asked Jesus.

" 'I am going to be crucified, Peter,' Jesus answered.

"Peter knew he could not allow Jesus to face His death alone; he could not abandon the Lord the way he had the first time. So Peter and his wife turned around and went back to Rome."

"Were they killed?" Tamar's voice was hard. She wished there could be another ending to her grandmother's story, but she was certain she already knew what had happened to Peter.

Grandma Mary nodded. "Yes, Child, they were. First, his wife was put to death, I heard, and how hard that must have been for Peter to watch! But he comforted his wife as she died. 'Remember the Lord!' he shouted. When it was his turn, they killed him on a cross, just as they had Jesus. But Peter, so they say, insisted he was not worthy to die the same way Jesus had. So they hung him on the cross upside down."

Tamar stared across the rooftop at the fig tree's branches. "Is that story supposed to make me feel better, Grandma?" She jumped to her feet and stood staring down at the frail old woman. "Well, it doesn't! And I still won't go to First Day worship. I don't want to be like Peter. I don't want to die for Jesus!"

Tamar spent the next few days pretending she didn't exist. When she went to draw water from the village well with the other girls, she ducked her head so that her mantle hid her face. She didn't speak to anyone unless they spoke to her. If she acted as though she were invisible, she reasoned, maybe no one would notice her. And if no one noticed her, she would give no one any reason to accuse her of being a Christian.

But one day as she walked quickly through the village marketplace, a bucket of water sloshing in each hand, she heard a commotion behind her. With a sinking in her heart, she recognized her brother's voice. Her steps slowed, and she darted a glance over her shoulder to see what was going on.

Lamech the smith had grabbed Daniel by the neck of his robe and was shouting at him. "What business is it of yours what I charge for my work?" Tamar heard him say.

Daniel had two red spots high on his cheekbones, but he held himself very straight. With a sigh, Tamar turned around and inched closer to hear what was going on.

"That woman is a widow," Daniel was saying. "You have no right to cheat her out of her money like that."

Lamech growled deep in his throat. "And why is that

your concern, Boy?" With his thick fist, he gave Daniel a shake that lifted the boy's sandals off the ground. "Oh, now I understand." Lamech thrust his bearded face close to Daniel's. "I know who you are. You belong to Mary Magdalene's family. You're one of those Christians. People who don't know enough to mind their own business." Lamech abruptly let go of Daniel's robe, and the boy stumbled backward. Lamech spat on the ground in disgust, then turned back to his work. "Go on," he snarled over his shoulder. "I won't see you around my workshop again—not if you know what's good for you."

Tamar gulped back the fear in her throat and hurried to her brother's side. "Are you all right?" she whispered.

He was very pale, but he nodded. Then his eyes narrowed as he looked at his sister's frightened face. "I am surprised you're willing to be seen in public with me," he hissed. Without another word, he turned on his heel and strode away from her.

Tamar gazed after him for a moment, but then she realized that the crowd around her was still murmuring about Lamech and Daniel. She shifted the buckets' weight in her hands and hurried across the marketplace.

When she reached her home, she found her mother making bread in the courtyard. Her mother looked up as Tamar set the water at her feet.

"Thank you." She looked into her daughter's face and

hesitated. "Is something wrong, Tamar?" she asked after a moment.

Tamar opened her mouth to tell about the incident between Lamech and Daniel, but then she closed her lips. What good would it do to tell her mother? Within their church, her mother was considered a leader, and Tamar knew the others respected her and looked up to her; but outside their small group of Christians, Mother was only a woman, with no man to protect her. She could do nothing to stop angry men like Lamech from making trouble for Daniel. Tamar sighed. No, her mother could do nothing to protect any of them from Emperor Trajan's cruel law.

Her mother turned back to the dough she was kneading. "Why don't you go visit Grandma Mary?" she suggested.

Tamar stuck out her lip. "I don't want to," she muttered.

Her mother didn't even glance up from her work. "Go on," she said firmly. "Grandma Mary may need help with something. Besides, I'd feel better if you checked on her. I don't like her living all alone these days. Not with those stiff joints of hers. One of these days, she's going to fall." Her mother scratched her eyebrow, leaving a streak of flour across her face. "Go on now, Tamar. Make sure she's all right. Ask her if she wants to eat supper with us tonight."

Only a few months ago, Tamar would have been delighted to visit Grandma Mary, but lately her great-grandmother made her feel uncomfortable. All her stories about the Master. . . And everyone in the village knew Grandma Mary was a Christian. Couldn't Mother see it was dangerous for them to spend too much time with Grandma Mary now? Tamar turned to do as her mother had asked, but her feet were slow and reluctant as she walked down the short alley that led to her grandmother's small house.

She found Grandma Mary sitting in the sunlight outside her door, spinning flax into thread. Her eyes lit up when she saw Tamar. "There you are, Child. I was just speaking with the Master about you. How are you today?"

"All right," Tamar mumbled. Then she met Grandma Mary's bright gaze. "No, I'm not all right," she burst out. "Daniel is going to get us all in trouble. Today he made Lamech the smith angry in the marketplace. Why can't Daniel just keep his mouth shut?"

Grandma Mary laughed. "The last time we spoke, Child, you reminded me of Peter. But I declare, today you sound more like Andrew." She patted the space beside her on the wooden bench. "Come, sit down. Let me tell you about another of the Lord's disciples. Maybe Andrew's story will help you with your own problems."

Tamar bit her lip, fighting the temptation to offer her grandmother an excuse and escape. Then she sighed and dropped down on the bench. "Oh, all right. Tell me about Andrew."

"Andrew, as you know, was Simon Peter's brother. And Andrew grew up in his brother's shadow. Peter was the one whom people noticed; he was the one who was always getting into trouble; and he was the one who just couldn't keep his mouth shut. Andrew was quieter. When he was in a large group, he liked to just fade into the background. Some people thought he was a humbler person than his loud brother. But really, I think Andrew just figured the background was a safer place to be. He must have gotten pretty annoyed with his brother sometimes. Peter was one of those people who always think they know better than anyone else what everyone else ought to be doing—except Peter was usually the first one to land himself in trouble. Andrew must have gotten tired of always being dragged along into his brother's messes. But however Andrew felt about his brother before he met Jesus, all that changed once he met the Lord.

"A year or so before he met Jesus, Andrew had left the fishing business and followed John the Baptist. He was a quiet man, Andrew was, but once he committed himself to someone or something, he gave his whole self.

"Andrew learned a lot from listening to the teachings of John the Baptist, but John kept talking about someone else, his cousin, Jesus of Nazareth. 'Jesus,' John told Andrew, 'is far greater than I am, for He existed long before I did. He is the Lamb of God who takes away the sin of the world.' When John said those words, something stirred inside Andrew, a strange feeling of both joy and yearning.

" 'I want to meet this man,' he told John. 'Can you introduce me to Him?'

"So a few days later, as Andrew was talking with John the Baptist, John suddenly pointed at a man walking toward them. 'There He is!' John told Andrew. 'There is the Lamb of God, the one I told you about.'

"Andrew watched as Jesus walked past them without seeming to notice His cousin. That odd yearning feeling was back inside Andrew again, and suddenly he knew he couldn't bear just to stand there while Jesus walked away from him. Without another word to John the Baptist, Andrew ran after Jesus. And if I know John, he just grinned and shook his head. He knew he had only come to prepare the way for Jesus, and he never minded when people followed his cousin instead of him. That was his purpose in life—to point people toward the Lord.

"Well, Jesus must have heard footsteps behind Him, because pretty soon He turned around and saw Andrew running after Him. 'What do you want?' He asked.

"Andrew wasn't like Peter; his words didn't come to him easily. The only thing he could think to say was, 'Teacher, where are You staying?'

"Jesus smiled. 'Why don't you come and see?'

"So just like that, Andrew went with Jesus, and he spent the rest of the day talking with Him. Afterward, right away, he went to his brother to tell him he had found the Messiah, and he brought Peter back with him to Jesus.

"Andrew was like that, always quick to share anything good that he had. And when it came right down to it, he was always loyal to his brother. And like I said, once he gave his heart, he gave everything.

"We all saw it that time when the crowd of five thousand men and their families followed Jesus out into the hills. When Jesus asked Philip how they were going to feed all those people, the other disciples thought Jesus was joking. Some of them were downright exasperated with the Lord. But Andrew didn't laugh, and he didn't say a word of protest. Instead, he just turned around and quietly began going through the crowd, asking to see if anyone had any food they could share.

"After awhile, he came back to Jesus and the other disciples. 'A little boy has five loaves and two fishes, Master,' he said. 'That's all I could find.'

"The other disciples rolled their eyes; they thought Andrew was foolish even to mention such a small amount when there must have been more than fifteen thousand hungry people there. But Andrew didn't care if he looked foolish. He just looked at Jesus, waiting to see what He would say.

"Jesus smiled. 'Thank you, Andrew. Bring the boy to Me.' And then, of course, you know what happened next. Jesus took that tiny lunch, and He blessed it—and then He shared it with the crowd. And there was enough for every last man, woman, and child, with enough left over for Jesus and His friends.

"People still remember Peter more than they do his brother. But the miracle that happened that day would never have taken place without Andrew's faith in the Lord."

Grandma Mary's gnarled thumb and finger slid deftly over the smooth fiber as she spun the flax into linen thread. Without looking up from her work, she smiled. "So you see, Child, you aren't the only one with a loud brother who jumps into trouble before he thinks. But the Lord has a place and a purpose for both of you in His kingdom."

Tamar leaned her elbows on her knees and scowled down at her dusty toes. "But did Peter put Andrew in danger?" she asked. "In the end, did Andrew end up getting killed by the Romans, just like his brother?"

Grandma Mary dropped her hands into her lap and was silent for a moment. "I lost touch with Andrew after Pentecost," she said thoughtfully, "but I heard tell that Andrew continued to serve the Lord in his own way for the next thirty or more years. While Peter was busy being an important leader of the church, Andrew just kept quietly introducing more and more people to Jesus, the same way he had so many years ago with Peter. I heard that Andrew traveled to Scythia and Armenia and Greece, telling everyone about the good news of Jesus."

"So is he still alive?" Tamar asked.

Her grandmother smiled. "No, I heard he died years ago."

Tamar sucked in a breath. "Was he killed by the Romans?"

"In a way," Grandma Mary said softly. "He was in Patrae, a city in Greece. The wife of the governor there heard Andrew speaking of Jesus; and she, too, became a Christian. But her husband was furious. So he had Andrew arrested and thrown into prison."

She smiled again, though Tamar could see no reason why she would think the story was funny.

"Why are you smiling?" she asked, her voice hard.

"What? Oh, I was just remembering something I heard. It seems that the governor couldn't keep his prison guards once Andrew was in the prison. One after another, the guards would get to know Andrew—and then they would quit their jobs, because they had given their hearts to Jesus."

"So did the governor let Andrew go?"

Grandma Mary shook her head, and her smile faded. "No. I heard that the governor became so frustrated he ordered that Andrew be put on a cross down by the shore. He had Andrew tied to the boards instead of nailed, so that Andrew would die a slow, painful death from exposure and thirst. Finally, though, the governor relented and had Andrew cut down off the cross, but by this time it was too late. Andrew was an old man by now, and his body could not recover from the terrible experience. He died at the governor's feet, lying there beside the sea."

"That's horrible!" Tamar spit out.

Her grandmother nodded. "Yes, it is. But listen to what Andrew said before he died: 'Jesus Christ, Whom I have seen, Whom I have, Whom I love, in Whom I am and will be, receive me in peace. Use my life so that all those who identify with me may rest in Your majesty.' " Grandma Mary looked into Tamar's face. "Does that sound like such a terrible way to die, Child?"

Tamar looked away from her grandmother's bright eyes. "Andrew may have had an obnoxious brother like Daniel—but I'm nothing like Andrew, either."

"Are you sure about that, Child?" Grandma Mary touched Tamar's hand. "How do you know who you will be if you open your heart to Jesus?"

CHAPTER 4

In spite of herself, all through the rest of that day, Tamar kept hearing her grandmother's question inside her head: *How do you know who you will be if you open your heart to Jesus?* She tried to tell herself that the question was a silly one; after all, how could you open your heart to someone Who had died nearly seventy years ago?

To make matters worse, the next day her mother and Grandma Mary decided to do the yearly dyeing; this meant Tamar would be working with her mother and great-grandmother from early in the morning until nightfall as together they dipped skeins of linen thread into the dyeing vats and hung them up to dry. Like always, Grandma Mary would, no doubt, be full of stories.

Once, Tamar had loved to sit and listen to her grandmother's stories, but now they made her uncomfortable. She knew Grandma Mary was hoping Tamar would choose to become a disciple of Jesus, just as Peter and Andrew and all the others had. Instead, Tamar wanted to plug her ears with her fingers to keep out her grandmother's words. *I have nothing in common with those twelve men,* she told herself. *Nothing at all.*

As Grandma Mary stirred a vat of scarlet dye, she began

to talk. Tamar bent over her work and pretended not to listen. *I'm not like you and Mother and Daniel,* she wanted to shout. *And I don't want to be like you. I don't care about loving my enemies, and I don't want to give my life for Jesus or anyone else. I just want to be free. I hate the Romans. I wish I could kill them all. I wish Emperor Trajan would die a horrible death, so he could never hurt anyone again. . . .*

But her angry, rebellious thoughts couldn't shut out her grandmother's voice as she began to tell about two more of Jesus' friends. In spite of herself, Tamar began to listen.

"Simon and Jude (or Thaddaeus, as some call him) hated the Romans." Grandma Mary threw a sharp glance at Tamar's stormy face and smiled. "In fact, their whole lives were ruled by their hatred. They both belonged to a group of rebels called the Zealots, and this group was determined that Israel would once more be a free nation.

"The Zealots would have done anything to overthrow the Romans' power. They were willing to die for our nation. And they were also willing to murder.

"Simon and Jude were first drawn to Jesus because they thought He was the answer to their dreams of freedom. After all, Jesus claimed to be a King, the Messiah, the Savior. Simon and Jude assumed He meant He would rule Israel instead of Herod, the evil servant of Rome. They expected Jesus to save His nation from Rome's power.

"Simon and Jude couldn't help but be puzzled by Jesus' methods, though. For instance, under any other circumstances they would never have put up with Matthew, who had been a tax collector. The Zealots hated tax collectors, since they were the servants of Rome, and without Jesus' influence, Simon and Jude would have rather killed Matthew than be his friend. But they believed in Jesus enough that they swallowed their hatred, although for a long time I think they kept a suspicious eye on Matthew.

"And as they spent time with Jesus, little by little they understood that when Jesus spoke of saving His people, He meant something far different than they did. His kingdom was an eternal one that had nothing to do with this world's rulers, and He intended to save everyone, not just the Jews, from something far bigger than the Romans. It was a hard concept for them to grasp, but finally both Jude and Simon realized that Jesus was the Savior of the world. He had come to bridge the separation between God and human beings. Jesus' purpose on earth was to bring us the good news that we could live forever with Him in His eternal kingdom.

"But even on the night before Jesus' death, when He ate His last supper with His disciples, Jude was still having trouble understanding Jesus' purpose. So he asked the Lord, 'It's all very well for You to tell us that You are the Messiah, the Chosen One of God. We understand that now. But isn't it time for You to show everyone else? Hasn't the time come for You to demonstrate Your power to the world at large?'

"Jude was still thinking like a rebel. He wanted Jesus to dazzle and impress people into faith. But Jesus knew that no power, no matter how great, can be a substitute for love.

" 'All those who love Me will do what I say anyway,' He told Jude. 'And if they love Me and follow Me, My Father will love them, and We will come to them and live with them.' He shook His head ruefully. 'It wouldn't matter how many miracles I did. Anyone who does not love Me will still not do what I say.' He smiled at Jude and then He turned to the other disciples. 'I am leaving you with a gift—peace of mind and heart. And the peace I give isn't like the peace the world gives. So don't be troubled or afraid.' "

Grandma Mary smiled as though she were still remembering her old friends. "Simon and Jude were with us at Pentecost when we were filled with the Holy Spirit's power. Like all of us, they were changed after that. Their doubts and questions and misunderstandings were gone, and they finally realized what Jesus had been trying to tell them.

"Now they were no longer filled with hatred. Instead, they were overflowing with love. They became two of our greatest missionaries, and together they traveled all over the world, carrying the good news of Christ. Eventually, they went to the nation of Persia, bringing the gospel to those who live there."

Grandma Mary sighed. "And yes, I know what you are going to ask next, Child. They were indeed killed for their faith. I heard that their enemies set an angry mob of people on them." The old woman smiled. "But I heard that Simon and Jude were not afraid. They watched as the crowd drew nearer, pelting them with stones, and then Jude turned to Simon and calmly remarked, 'I see that the Lord is calling us.'

"The two men were killed by the mob. But don't you see, Child, that even then the power of hatred did not win? Nothing can prevail against the love of God."

CHAPTER 5

When First Day came, to Tamar's surprise her mother acted as though she assumed that Tamar would stay home. Even Daniel said good-bye to her and nothing more.

Once he and their mother left the house, Tamar wandered out into the courtyard. She felt strange being home all alone. At first, she told herself she was enjoying the peace and quiet, but as the hours passed, she began to feel more and more lonely.

If only she had a friend she could talk with. Lately, though, she was afraid to talk to the other girls her age for fear they would ask her about being a Christian. Besides, she had noticed that the girls avoided her when they saw her in the marketplace or at the well, as though they knew it might be dangerous for them to be seen with her.

Tamar's eye filled with tears. "I miss Flavia," she whispered to the empty courtyard. "I wish I had a friend."

She thought of the other Christians who would be together now at the house of Alexander and Perpetua. They would be singing psalms or reading from one of the letters from the apostle Paul; by now they might be praying or sharing the Lord's meal. At least they had each other, Tamar realized. Sitting all alone in the quiet morning, she felt like an outcast who didn't belong anywhere.

When she heard the voices of her mother and Daniel out in the street, she was so relieved that she jumped up and ran to meet them. They had brought Grandma Mary home with them, and the old woman looked up into Tamar's face. "Were you lonely, Child?" she asked softly.

Tamar refused to answer her great-grandmother, but the old woman seemed to read the truth in Tamar's eyes. "You make me think of my old friend Matthew," Grandma Mary said. She patted Tamar's arm. "Come, Child. Sit with me a moment, and let me tell you about another of the Lord's disciples."

"Matthew was also called Levi, you know. But whatever he was called, people hated him.

"Many of the Lord's twelve followers were fishermen and other types of workingmen—but Matthew didn't get his hands dirty with honest labor. No, before Matthew became the Lord's disciple, he was a tax collector. He worked for the Romans, collecting the money they squeezed out of his fellow Jews. Or rather he worked for the Romans' servant, the evil Herod Antipas, which was even worse. Matthew's work made him a rich man, with a comfortable home where he hosted lavish feasts. But his work also made him a despised man.

"Matthew was the brother of James, another of Jesus'

disciples, so I wouldn't be surprised if Jesus had known Matthew since they were both boys. Matthew had talked with Jesus and questioned Him and discussed His ideas about God for years. But when Jesus made Him one of His Twelve, people still talked and whispered. The religious leaders were especially angry that Jesus would call a man who had grown rich by cheating his own people.

"But the opinion of others never stopped Jesus. In fact, He made a practice of eating with tax collectors and sinners and people like me, Mary Magdalene. We were all people with whom anyone else would never have dared to be seen.

"So one day, when Jesus walked by and saw Matthew sitting at his work, Jesus stopped. He looked at Matthew for a moment, and then He said simply, 'Follow Me.'

"And that was all it took. Whatever conversations had gone before between the two of them, by this time Matthew was ready. For all his great wealth, he was probably tired of feeling lonely and outcast. Just like that, he got up from his work and walked away. He followed Jesus. And he never turned back.

"The first thing Matthew did after he became Jesus' disciple was to invite Jesus to a feast in his home. Matthew invited the only friends he had, other tax collectors and outcasts; he wanted everyone to have the chance to meet Jesus, just as he had.

"The religious leaders were shocked and horrified that

Jesus would eat with such an assortment of 'worthless' people. They took the Lord's other disciples aside and asked them, 'Why do you eat with such scum?'

"But Jesus told them, 'Healthy people don't need a doctor—sick people do. I have come to call sinners to turn from their sins, not to spend My time with those who think they are already good enough.'

"You see, Jesus had looked into Matthew's heart, just as He had with Peter, He saw the person God had created Matthew to be. Jesus didn't care what a person looked like on the outside; He knew that Matthew the tax collector had a disciple hidden deep inside him, a disciple Jesus needed to build His kingdom.

"And Matthew had skills the kingdom needed as well. Unlike many of the other disciples, he knew how to read and write. After the Lord's death, Matthew collected the stories and sayings of Jesus. He wrote them down, edited them, and added some of his own memories of the Lord. Today Phineus read to us from Matthew's story.

"I lost touch with Matthew years ago. The last I knew he was still traveling around the world, spreading the good news that God's Son came to earth to bring us all to heaven.

"But whatever happened to Matthew and wherever he went, I know he never felt like an outcast again. He had found a Friend who would never leave him, no matter what. And through Jesus, Matthew now belonged to the entire body of believers."

Grandma Mary smiled at her granddaughter. "You see, Child, we need never be lonely again. Not when we have Jesus and each other."

CHAPTER 6

As quickly as she could, Tamar slipped away from Grandmother and went to help her mother lay out the evening meal. If only her family would just leave her alone!

Her mother said nothing to Tamar about her decision to stay home again from the First Day gathering, but as they gathered around the table to eat, Daniel began to tease Tamar for not joining with the others for the Lord's meal. Finally, Tamar lost her temper. When her mother asked her to serve Daniel a bowl of figs, Tamar dropped them on his head instead.

"You may leave the table, Tamar," her mother said quietly. "When you are ready to apologize to your brother, you may return."

"What about him—?" Tamar began, but her mother cut her off with one quick movement of her hand.

"Go sit in the courtyard until your temper has cooled, Tamar."

While the others finished their meal, Tamar used a stick to draw lines in the dusty earth. After a moment, a shadow fell across her, and she looked up to see her great-grandmother.

Tamar sighed. "See, Grandma? I'm not like the disciples

at all. I lose my temper far too easily to ever follow Jesus. You might as well give up on me."

Her grandmother sat down beside her on the stone step. For a moment, the old woman rubbed her sore legs with her hands, and then, as her pain eased, she sighed. "Child, a bad temper is no excuse for not following Jesus." Her eyes grew misty and faraway, as though she were once more remembering her old friends. "Let me tell you about John and James," she said.

"Today, John and James are famous for being loving leaders of our church. But Jesus called the two brothers the 'Sons of Thunder.' They had nasty tempers, you see, and they were proud, ambitious men who stormed and stomped when things didn't go their way. John especially didn't have much patience with people who didn't do things right.

"The two brothers' mother was Salome, and Salome was the sister of Jesus' mother, so the three boys had grown up knowing each other. Some say that was why John was one of Jesus' closest friends. But I think it was more than that. Despite his arrogance and impatience, John understood Jesus' mission on earth. He had spent so much time with the Lord that he knew Jesus' kingdom stretched far beyond this physical world.

"John and James were the sons of old Zebedee, Peter and Andrew's fishing partner, and like their father, John and

James were fishermen. They were not poor, uneducated laborers, though, because Zebedee was a successful fish merchant, a wealthy man with servants. It may be that at first John and James thought they were better than some of the other disciples because of their family connection to Jesus and because of their family's wealth and importance. After all, Zebedee even had connections with the high priest.

"One day, when John and James were mending their fishing nets with their father, Jesus came walking along the shore. 'Come follow Me,' He shouted.

"John and James must have known that Jesus was ready now to begin His ministry. For all their pride, the two brothers loved Jesus enough that when Jesus called, they answered. Without asking a single question, the two brothers jumped up, leaving their nets and their fishing boat behind, and from that day on they followed the Lord.

"But that didn't mean they changed overnight into the sort of people God wanted them to be. No, just like the rest of us, James and John still had faults they struggled with. They still thought they were the center of the world—or at least they thought they ought to be!

"So because they felt that way, one day they took Jesus aside. 'Jesus,' they said, 'we want You to do us a favor.'

" 'What is it?' Jesus asked them.

" 'Well,' they said, 'when we all enter Your glorious

kingdom, we want to sit in places of honor next to You—one of us at Your right side and the other on Your left. After all, we're Your closest friends, aren't we?'

"But Jesus looked sad and shook His head. 'You don't know what you're asking,' He told them. 'Are you able to drink from the bitter cup of sorrow I am about to drink? Are you able to be baptized with the baptism of suffering I must be baptized with?'

"John and James didn't even hesitate; they were so confident of themselves. 'Oh, yes,' they said, 'we are able.'

"Jesus looked at them for a long moment, as though He was seeing all the way inside their hearts. And then He said, "You will indeed drink from My cup and be baptized with My baptism. But I have no right to say who will sit on the thrones next to Mine. God has prepared those places for the ones He has chosen.'

"You see Jesus knew that John and James would have to give themselves away before they could really rule in His kingdom. They would have to give up thinking of themselves as the center of the world. And that always hurts.

"Of course, the other disciples were angry when they heard what James and John had asked of Jesus. 'Who do they think they are?' they muttered. 'What gives them the right to expect to rule in Jesus' kingdom?'

"But Jesus called them all together and told them, 'Things work a little differently in My kingdom, fellows. If you want to be a leader in the kingdom of God, then you must first give your lives in serving others. And if you want to be first, then you have to lay down your lives in love. For even I, the Son of Man, came here not to be served but to serve others, and to give My life as a ransom for many.'

"James and John were beginning to get the picture—but they still had a lot to learn, as we could all see one day when they overheard someone casting out demons in Jesus' name. John especially was all upset that this stranger would dare to call on Jesus' power, and John immediately ran off to tell Jesus, just like a kid tattling on another child.

" 'Master,' John said, 'we saw someone using Your name to cast out demons. We tried to stop him because he wasn't in our group.'

"He looked as though he expected Jesus to praise him for what he had done, but instead, Jesus looked stern. 'Don't stop anyone who is doing good in My name! Anyone who is not against us is for us.'

"You see, James and John still thought they were better than everyone else, that they had some sort of inside advantage simply because they were in Jesus' circle of close friends. Jesus had to keep telling them and telling them that things don't work that way in His kingdom. In the kingdom of heaven there are no insiders and outsiders; in fact, in the kingdom, there is no distinction based on whether you're a slave or a king, a man or a woman, a rich man or a beggar. The smallest, poorest, weakest child who opens her heart to Jesus belongs just as much the biggest, richest, strongest man.

"But James and John still hadn't really grasped what Jesus was all about, because pretty soon, when the disciples and Jesus were traveling through Samaria on their way to Jerusalem, they ran into some trouble at a village that refused to welcome Jesus and His friends. John and James were so angry they wanted to call down fire from heaven and destroy the entire village.

"But again, Jesus just looked at them and shook His head. 'You don't realize what your hearts are like when you think things like this. Don't you understand yet? I didn't come to destroy people's lives but to save them.'

"From all I've said, you might think that James and John were stuck-up, unlikable fellows. And they could be, I have to admit. Still, we all loved them, and Jesus seemed to see past their faults. He loved them and He liked being with them; sometimes when He was tired and needed some rest, He would go off with just James and John and Peter for some peace and relaxation.

"And little by little, as James and John grew closer and closer to the Lord, they began to change. Oh, they still had their faults. They were never very patient with others, and they were always thinking that everyone else's mistakes should be punished far more severely than their own. But they loved Jesus with their whole hearts. Jesus knew He could count on them.

"So when Jesus hung dying from the cross, He looked down at all of us who were standing below. It broke my heart to see Him suffering like that, but even then Jesus was thinking of others. He looked at His good friend John standing beside His own mother Mary, and He said, 'From now on she is your mother.'

"Mary's husband Joseph had died years ago, and Jesus knew that, the way our world was, she would need someone to provide for her when He was gone. So from that day on, John took Mary into his own home and cared for her until she died.

"And James and John proved they could drink from Jesus' cup, because they no longer tried to be the center of the world. From then on, they gave themselves away in Jesus' name."

Tamar sniffed. "I suppose you mean they were killed by the Romans."

Grandma Mary smiled. "There are all sorts of ways to give your life for Jesus, Child. James was the first of the twelve disciples who were put to death; Herod had him killed with a sword. But my old friend John is still alive today, though he's even older than I am. He lives in Ephesus, and the last I heard, he was still preaching the good news.

He's nearly a hundred years old now, and he's grown very weak, so that his friends have to carry him to the First Day services. When he gets there and stands before them, he always says the very same thing: 'Little children, love one another.' "

Grandma Mary laughed to herself. "I've heard lately that people are complaining because John has grown so old he always preaches the very same sermon. But when John hears them grumbling, he just laughs and says, 'Love is the Lord's command. If we do that and nothing else, we will have done enough.'

"So you see, Child, John didn't need to be killed by the Romans to give his life completely away to Jesus. Instead, he has lived his long life in his Lord's service. And," she smiled into Tamar's eyes, "Jesus can take someone with a bad temper and turn them into someone who lives for Him."

CHAPTER 7

When the next First Day came, Tamar reluctantly went with her family to the worship service. She didn't want to spend the day alone again; but she didn't want to be at church, either. While all the others were singing and praying and reading from the Psalms and the Gospel stories, Tamar was listening for the heavy steps of soldiers outside the door. When the others gathered to share the Lord's meal, their faces full of joy and peace, Tamar hung back. She didn't belong at the table, she knew, not when her heart was so full of anger and fear and doubt.

She knew her mother and Daniel believed in Jesus without question—that they were completely committed to His way of living. But sometimes Tamar wondered if they really, really believed that Jesus was still present with them. How could He be? Grandma Mary might believe He was, but she had known Jesus and loved Him. Sometimes Tamar wondered if Grandma had just convinced herself that Jesus was still alive so that she wouldn't have to face how much she missed Him.

Tamar shook her head as she watched the others bow their heads in prayer. No matter what Grandma Mary said, Tamar knew she was nothing like any of the disciples. She was too full of doubt ever to follow Jesus with the confidence of those brave men.

After the worship service was over, the family gathered at Grandma Mary's house to eat the evening meal. Grandma Mary said the blessing over the food, and then she glanced across the table at Tamar. "I've been thinking, Child. And I think I know which of the Lord's disciples you'd relate to most."

Tamar bit back a sigh. "Who is that, Grandma?"

Her grandmother clapped her hands with delight. "Someone who was just as full of doubts as you are. Thomas!" She took a bit of meat, and then she began her story.

"If you handed Thomas a cup of water that was half full, he was the sort of person who would only see the half that was empty. He believed in calling a spade a spade; and he figured if something bad might happen, then it probably would. While some of the other disciples had their heads full of fantasies about all the wonderful things that would happen once Jesus had set up His kingdom here on earth, Thomas had his feet firmly on the ground. He knew the world was full of danger, and he was fully prepared to stick by Jesus no matter what.

"He proved this the time when Lazarus died. Jesus had already run into some trouble from the religious leaders in Jerusalem—they had tried to stone Him twice—so when the disciples got word that Lazarus was dead, they didn't know why Jesus would want to go anywhere near Jerusalem. After all, it was too late to do Lazarus any good, and Jesus could end up getting them all killed as well.

"But Jesus insisted on going to the home of Lazarus's sisters, in Bethany just outside Jerusalem. The other disciples muttered and complained—but with a sigh, Thomas got to his feet to follow the Lord. 'Come on,' he said to the others. 'We might as well go and die with Him.'

"That was just the way Thomas was. He wasn't always the most fun man to have around—but he was the sort of person you'd want with you if things got rough. Thomas never backed down.

"And he also never pretended to be something he was not. If he had doubts, then he said so. If he had a question, then he spoke up and asked.

"So at the disciples' last supper with the Lord, Thomas was the one who asked an important question. Jesus had just said to His friends, 'Don't be troubled. You trust God; now trust Me. There are many rooms in My Father's home, and I am going to prepare a place for you. If this were not so, I would tell you plainly. When everything is ready, I will come and get you, so that you will always be with Me where I am. And you know where I am going and how to get there.'

"The other disciples would have let the moment go by—

but Thomas couldn't keep silent. 'No, Lord,' he blurted out, 'we don't know where You are going. We don't have any idea, so how can we know the way?'

"Jesus smiled at him. 'Thomas, I know you don't understand what is happening. That doesn't matter. Whatever happens, you have Me. And I am the Way and the Truth and the Life. If you follow Me, then you will find the Father.'

"Thomas believed the Lord's words, but after Jesus died on the cross, Thomas was grief-stricken. He wasn't surprised or shocked, like some of the other disciples were, but that didn't make his sorrow any less deep. He loved the Lord with all his heart, you see, and so he went off away from the other disciples to be alone with his sadness.

"And that is why he missed seeing Jesus when He first appeared to the other disciples after His resurrection from the dead. When Thomas heard that the others claimed to have seen the risen Jesus, he was sure they had lost their minds. He had seen what had happened that time with Lazarus, when Jesus insisted on going to Bethany; Thomas knew Jesus had brought Lazarus back from the dead. But Thomas couldn't bring himself to believe that Jesus could raise Himself from the dead, as well. That was just too strange.

"No, Thomas wasn't going to believe in the risen Lord— 'Not,' he said, 'unless I see the nail wounds in His hands, put my fingers in them, and place my hand into the wound in His side.' You see, like so many of us, Thomas had a hard time believing in anything he couldn't see or touch.

"But Jesus didn't hold Thomas's doubt against him. A few days later, the disciples were all gathered together inside a locked room, when suddenly Jesus was there in the middle of them. Thomas's mouth fell open. He just stood there, staring, while Jesus smiled at him and held out His hands.

" 'Here you go, Thomas. Put your finger here and see My hands. Put your hand into the wound in My side. Go ahead! Don't doubt anymore. Believe!'

"But Thomas didn't need to touch Jesus to know He was real. With tears in his eyes, his voice shaking, he said, 'My Lord and my God!'

"Jesus gave His doubting disciple a hug, and then He said, 'You believe because you have seen Me. Blessed are those who haven't seen Me and believe anyway.' "

Grandma Mary looked into Tamar's face. "I know, Child, it's easier for me to have faith in the Lord, because I saw Him. You never saw Him. Like Thomas, you suspect the good news of Jesus is just too good to be true. But if you can let go of your doubt and believe in Him, He will bless you for your faith."

Tamar looked down at her plate. "I don't think Jesus has good news for us, Grandma," she said. "I don't think it's good news at all." She picked up a piece of bread and fiercely tore it into tiny pieces. "If Jesus gets us all killed by the Romans, then His message sounds like pretty bad news to me."

She heard her brother make a noise of disgust, but Grandma Mary held up her hand for Daniel to be silent. Tamar blinked back the tears that threatened to spill out and said, "What happened to Thomas, Grandma Mary? Did he die like the others?"

Her grandmother shook her head. "I don't know for sure what happened to Thomas, Child. I heard that he traveled far to the East, taking the gospel to the lands there. He may have faced death there eventually at the hands of enemies as so many of us have—or he may be there still, telling others that Jesus is the way to God. I do not know. But I do know that alive or dead, he is safe in the Lord's hands. Don't you see yet, Child? Nothing, nothing at all, can ever separate us from Jesus."

Chapter 8

As they finished their meal, Daniel sighed loudly. "Why are you being so stubborn, Tamar? It's not that hard to understand." He shook his head angrily. "How you can refuse to eat at the Lord's table? I'd say you're more like Judas than any of the other disciples."

"Daniel," their mother said, her voice firm and reproving.

But Tamar squinted her eyes at her brother and nodded. "Maybe Daniel is right. Maybe I am like Judas." She glanced at her grandmother. "Why don't you tell us about him, Grandma? I'd like to hear about someone who didn't throw everything away for Jesus."

"People like to think of Judas as being pure evil." Grandma Mary sighed, a sad look on her face. "But he wasn't. Jesus chose Judas just like He chose the other disciples. Jesus must have looked into Judas's heart and seen all the potential for goodness and love that was there. He loved Judas.

"The other disciples accepted and trusted Judas as well. They put Judas in charge of the group's money, and no one ever thought to suspect that Judas would turn on Jesus, not even at the very end.

"But Jesus knew. He understood Judas the way the

rest of us didn't.

"Jesus knew that Judas, like Simon and Jude, was a rebel against the Romans' rule. Judas believed Jesus was the Messiah, but he thought Jesus was going to set up an earthly kingdom rather than a heavenly, eternal one. Judas believed that Jesus had been sent by God, that He had supernatural power—but he was counting on Jesus to use that power to overthrow the Romans.

"So as the months went by, and still Jesus did nothing to set up an earthly kingdom, Judas became more and more frustrated. All Jesus did was heal sick people and talk about loving the poor. He just wasn't practical enough for Judas.

"Judas was furious that time when Mary of Bethany anointed Jesus' feet with expensive perfume. To Judas, pouring perfume on someone's feet, even Jesus' feet, seemed like such a silly, wasteful thing to do. If Jesus cared so much about the poor, reasoned Judas, then Mary should have used the money she had spent on that perfume to give to people who were in need. The money would have at least done someone good that way.

"But Judas was missing the whole point of what Mary did. For Mary, that perfume was a sacrifice of love, an expression of her whole heart. Jesus understood that. But poor Judas, his own heart was so pinched and practical that he couldn't comprehend such an extravagant love.

"Little frustrations like that one kept piling up inside

Judas's mind. I wonder, too, if he wasn't a little jealous of Peter and John and James. Judas was one of the group's leaders, and yet he was never included in those intimate moments alone with Jesus. He must have felt angry that Jesus confided in those three and not in him, and his jealousy festered inside him.

"Jesus knew all this, and He still loved Judas. At Jesus' last supper with His friends, He gave Judas one more chance by sitting next to him at the table. Then Jesus warned His disciples that one of them would betray Him.

"They were upset, of course, and one by one they asked Him, 'I'm not the one, am I, Lord?'

"He told them, 'The one who just dipped his hand into the bowl with Me is the one who will betray Me.'

"The others hadn't noticed who that was, but Judas said softly into Jesus' ear, 'You don't mean me, do You, Master?'

"Jesus looked at him for a long, silent moment, and then He said, 'That's up to you, Judas.'

"I don't know what Judas was thinking. Maybe he was so angry and jealous that he wanted Jesus to die. Or maybe he thought that by forcing a confrontation between Jesus and the religious leaders, he could make Jesus take action. He had seen Jesus' power, and, practical man that Judas was, he may have assumed Jesus would use His supernatural strength to protect Himself and begin His rule on earth.

"Whatever his reasons, I think that at that moment Judas

made his choice. He shut his heart to the Lord, and he opened it to the power of evil. He said no to love and life, and he said yes to hatred and death.

"Jesus read Judas's answer in his eyes. 'Go on now,' Jesus said with a sigh. 'Hurry and do what you have to.'

"Judas must have known that Jesus knew what he was going to do. I wonder sometimes if Judas pretended to himself that because Jesus knew, that made his actions all right. Maybe he told himself that Jesus wanted him to set up a confrontation between Jesus and the leaders. But deep in his heart, he knew that he was betraying the Lord.

"He led the soldiers and the religious leaders to the Garden of Gethsemane where Jesus was praying, and then he went up to Jesus. 'Hello, Master!' he said and gave Jesus a kiss.

" 'Judas, how can you betray Me with a kiss?' Jesus asked him.

"If Judas hadn't fully understood what he was doing before, he did then when he looked into the Lord's face.

"But he still could have chosen to trust Jesus, even then. After all, Peter also denied Jesus—and yet Peter asked the Lord's forgiveness and went on to be one of the church's greatest leaders. Judas could have taken that path as well.

"Judas wanted to have his own way. He didn't want to surrender to the Lord. But the thing is, when we throw everything away for Jesus, He gives us the whole world in return.

In the end, Judas threw everything away, including his own life. He missed out on all the blessings the Lord longed to give him. He chose death."

Grandma Mary looked across the table at Tamar, and for once she was not smiling. Her face was very solemn.

"Are you like Judas, Tamar? Do you choose death? Or do you choose life?"

CHAPTER 9

As Tamar helped her mother make flour the next day, her grandmother's questions echoed in her mind. *Do you choose death? Or do you choose life?* At first the questions made her angry. All along, she had been the one who didn't want to risk her life, while the others seemed perfectly content to let the Romans come and kill them. So of course she chose life.

But as she bent over the stone mortar, grinding the wheat into flour, she found herself thinking again and again about Judas. In a way, she understood Judas's thinking better than she did the other disciples'. As she had listened to her grandmother's stories, sooner or later, the other disciples had stopped making sense to her. The longer they were with Jesus, the more they seemed to throw common sense to the wind. Only Judas had kept his wits. He had believed his way was right; he had thought he was choosing life.

But the path he had chosen had not led to life and joy at all. He had ended up alone and bitter and frightened. . .and dead. Tamar felt fear touch her like a cold finger against her neck. She looked up at her mother's serene face as she worked, then across the courtyard to where Daniel was tending the donkey. They would never forsake Jesus, she knew, and if she refused to be around the other Christians, eventually she would lose her own family. She felt as though something was pinching her heart. "I don't want to lose you," she whispered.

Her mother looked up from her work. "What did you say, Tamar?"

Tamar flushed. "Nothing."

Her mother looked at her thoughtfully for a moment. Then she said, "You've done enough for now, Tamar. Your arms must be tired. Why don't you run over and check on Grandma Mary?"

Tamar hesitated. On the one hand, she dreaded hearing yet another of her grandmother's stories. But there was something she wanted to ask Grandma Mary. She put down the pestle and stood up. "All right," she sighed.

"Take her some of that fresh cheese," her mother called over her shoulder.

Tamar found her great-grandmother sitting up on her roof, her face tipped up to the sky.

"You shouldn't come up here by yourself, Grandma," Tamar scolded. "What if you fell on the steps?"

"Then I would wait for you to find me, Child." The old woman smiled. "This is where I feel closest to my Lord. When I talk to Him here, I can almost hear His answer." She tugged at Tamar's robe, pulling her down beside her. "Look how blue the sky is, Tamar."

Tamar looked up at the cloudless sky, and then she leaned back against the railing beside her grandmother. They sat together silently for a long moment, and Tamar felt some of the tension that had filled her for so long begin to seep out of her, as though it were draining into the deep blue dome above her head. When she let her breath out, she felt as though she had been holding it for weeks.

"I'm confused, Grandma," she said.

Her grandmother turned toward her but said nothing, merely waiting.

Tamar struggled to put her thoughts into words. "I don't want to be like Judas, Grandma. But Peter and John and Andrew and all the others. . .they were special. I can see that God must have been with them, but they were leaders. God needed them, or the church would never have spread and grown the way it did. I'm not like them. . .I'm just ordinary. So why would God care whether I followed Jesus or not? I'm not important to His kingdom." She searched her grandmother's lined face. "Why are you trying so hard to persuade me to follow Jesus? Why does it matter?"

Her grandmother was silent for a moment, and once again, Tamar had the uneasy feeling the old woman was talking to Jesus inside her head. Finally, Grandma Mary said, "There are two disciples I haven't mentioned so far,

Child. Let me tell you about them, and then maybe you will understand."

Tamar tipped her head back and looked up at the blue sky. "All right, Grandma. I'll listen to one more story."

"People know that Jesus had twelve disciples, but they always forget about two of them—James, the son of Alphaeus, and Nathanael (who was also called Bartholomew). These men were quiet people. They weren't leaders. They never did anything that made them stand out. But Jesus chose them just the same.

"James, the son of Alphaeus, was the brother of Matthew the tax collector. I have to confess, I know little more than that about him. I know he followed the Lord faithfully, but somehow nothing he did ever seemed particularly noteworthy.

"I know only a little more about Nathanael. He was the one whom Philip brought to Jesus. Like Philip and the others, Nathanael was a fisherman. He was a pious Jew who longed for the Messiah to come and deliver His people from the Romans' rule. One day, Nathanael took some time off from his work and sat in his courtyard under a fig tree, praying to God about the Messiah.

"And it was then that his friend Philip came to call and told him about Jesus of Nazareth. Nathanael answered, 'Can anything good come from that town?' Nathanael was from

Cana, a neighboring village, and apparently he knew some Nazarenes whom he didn't like.

"But Nathanael didn't let his prejudices stop him from meeting Jesus. He got up and went at once with Philip to meet the Lord.

"When Jesus saw them coming, He said, 'Here comes an honest man—a true son of Israel.'

"Nathanael was surprised. 'How do You know me?'

"Jesus smiled. 'I could see you under the fig tree this morning, Nathanael.'

For a moment, Nathanael was dumbstruck. Then he cried, "Teacher, You are the Son of God—the King of Israel!'

Jesus laughed. "You believe all that just because I told you I saw you under the fig tree? You will see greater things than this." His smile faded, and He looked deep into Nathanael's eyes. "The truth is, Nathanael, you will all see heaven open and the angels of God going up and down to the Son of Man.'

"So you see, in Jesus' eyes it didn't matter whether history would remember Nathanael. The Lord knew that Nathanael and quiet James would be there with the others in His eternal kingdom.

"I have heard stories that Nathanael (or Bartholomew, as he is often called) went on to travel the world with the gospel story of joy and love. I don't know whether those stories are true or not. But about ten years ago, I met a woman in the marketplace, a widow like me, who told me a story about both Nathanael and quiet James.

"The woman told me of something that had happened years before. Back then, she had been so poor she could not buy food for her son. She was a proud woman, who had once been the wife of a wealthy man, but the man's older son by a first wife had inherited all his riches. Now, to her shame, she was forced to go to the marketplace and beg. The crowd ignored her, however; no one stopped to give her even a penny, and as the hours passed, her shame turned to bitterness and despair. If her son had not needed her, she would have taken her own life.

"And then, just when her heart was brimming over with weariness and sorrow, two men stopped beside her. They questioned her kindly about her circumstances, and they told her about their Master, Jesus of Nazareth. Then they gave her enough money that she could go and buy bread to last for that day and many days after, enough for herself and her son. Before they left, she asked them their names, and she never forgot them.

"Because of those two soft-spoken men, this woman went home and told her son about Jesus. Nothing else much changed in their lives; they were still desperately poor. But somehow, the woman had hope now.

"And when her son grew up, he, too, followed Jesus. His mother told me that today he is spreading the gospel in a land far to the West. Because of him, a whole nation will come to know our Lord.

"So you see, the kingdom of heaven's history will look far different than this world's. In the light of eternity, that small simple act of kindness performed by James and Nathanael may be just as important as all the great sermons preached by Peter. The Lord knew what He was doing when He called those two quiet men to be His disciples."

Grandma Mary stretched her stiff legs, then rubbed her knees with a tiny moan. Tamar saw her grandmother's face grow tight with pain, but when she turned to her granddaughter, she was smiling.

"The Lord wants you to be His disciple, Tamar," she said softly.

"How do you know?"

"Because, Child, He needs each of us. We are all precious to Him, and we each have a role to play in His kingdom, just as each of the twelve disciples did. He may ask you to do something bold and marvelous in His name, something the world will remember centuries from now. Or He may simply need you to give water to the thirsty and a smile and a kind word to the lonely. Either way, it's all the same to Him."

The old woman took Tamar's hand in her gnarled fingers. "I heard once that each small act of kindness vibrates forever through the kingdom of heaven. The person who started this echo of love could never have guessed how lives would be changed centuries from now on the other side of the world. Each kindness performed for the kingdom is passed on and grows each time it's passed, until a simple courtesy may inspire some stupendous act of selfless courage years later and miles away. The kingdom's walls are built of tiny stones—but oh, Child, how those stones shine! And how tall those walls grow when we are each faithful to lay our small measure down on Christ, the foundation stone of it all!"

Tamar frowned. "I'm still not sure I understand."

Grandma Mary laughed. "Of course not, Child. None of us does. We can only catch glimmers from Jesus' eternal kingdom. But we don't need to understand. All we have to do is keep our eyes on the Lord."

Tamar clung to her grandmother's hand. "But I'm still scared. What if the Romans kill us?"

Grandma Mary looked up at the sky. "We cannot predict the future, Child. When I was young, I expected to die for my Lord, as so many of my friends had. And yet here I still am, an old woman who has been allowed to live my life in peace." She rubbed her legs and grimaced. "Sometimes I wonder if dying for the Lord when I was young might have been easier than living with this constant pain in my legs."

She turned to look at her granddaughter. "You see, Child,

each life holds a measure of pain and sorrow. That's simply the way life is on this earth. No matter what choice you make now, you cannot escape this world's shadows. Eventually, sooner or later, one way or the other, they will catch up with you."

Her small, wrinkled face lit up with joy. "But when we follow the Lord, Child, He fills our lives with joy and love and untold blessings. When the hard times come, we never have to face them alone, for He is always with us. Once you open your heart to Him, like the disciples, you will know His peace, His happiness, His love. And then, whatever comes, it will all be worth it to you."

She struggled painfully to her feet. "I will leave you alone now, Child. Talk to the Lord. See if you hear His voice."

Tamar held her breath as her grandmother climbed slowly down the stairs. When the old woman was safely on the ground once more, Tamar looked up again at the sky. She sat quietly for a long time, thinking about all that Grandma Mary had told her.

"Jesus?" Tamar whispered at last.

She heard no answer from the blue sky above her head. But suddenly, for the first time in weeks, her heart leapt with joy. "Jesus?" she asked again, her eyes wide with wonder.

And then she bowed her head against her bent knees. "I want to be Your disciple, Lord."

If you enjoyed

THE SON OF GOD,

check out these other great
Backpack Books!